Oct 2000

To Sylvia,

With warmest affection

Bill

Jews and Mormons: Two Houses of Israel

Jews and Mormons: Two Houses of Israel

by

Frank J. Johnson

and

Rabbi William J. Leffler

Ktav Publishing House, Inc.
Hoboken, NJ

Copyright©2000
Frank J. Johnson and William J. Leffler
Library of Congress Cataloging-in-Publication-Data
Johnson, Frank., 1930-
    Jews and Mormons : two houses of Israel / by Frank J. Johnson and William J. Leffler.
        p. cm
    Includes bibliographical references.
    ISBN 0-88125-689-7
    1. Mormon Church --Relations--Judaism. 2. Judaism--Relations -- Morman Church. 3.
Mormon Church--Doctrines. 4. Jews--Restoration. I. Leffler, William J. II. Title.

BX8643.J84 J64 2000
296.3'.96--dc21

                                                                    00-042812
                                                                    CIP

Manufactured in the United States of America
Distributed by
Ktav Publishing House, Inc.
900 Jefferson Street
Hoboken, NJ 07030
(201) 963-9524 Fax (201) 963-0101
Ktav@compuserve.com

Table of Contents

Acknowledgments

I want to thank Rabbis Simeon Maslin, Richard Safran and Leonard Schoolman for reading and critiquing the manuscript, and Rabbi A. James Rudin for his words of encouragement. I also want to thank Donna McLean, our agent for her diligence, patience, perseverence and support. And lastly, my wife, Ki, for her encouragement and willingness to lose me to many hours of work on the manuscript.

— Rabbi William J. Leffler

I wish to particularly thank Brian Johnson for his review of my text and his excellent suggestions for clarification and improvement; Ken and Sharlene Bentley for their input to my portion of Chapter nine; Glenn Potter for his many hours at the computer helping me to organize the manuscript. They are good friends all and I am grateful for their help. My wife Sally has also contributed significantly to this work as advocate and critic; she has been a constant inspiration.

In a broader sense I want to thank all of those Latter-day Saints who provided enthusiastic moral support for this project to bring greater understanding between Jews and Mormons. I hope that they will be pleased by the efforts of Rabbi Leffler and myself to bring this about.

— Frank J. Johnson

Preface

Jews and Mormons: Two Houses of Israel is the combined effort of Frank J. Johnson, a Mormon High Priest, and William J. Leffler, a retired Reform rabbi. Mr. Johnson, a convert to the Church of Jesus Christ of Latter-day Saints (also known as the Mormon Church), is soon to reside in Mesa, Arizona. In 1994–95 he spent a year with his wife as a full-time missionary in the Canada Toronto-East Mission. Rabbi Leffler held congregational pulpits in Concord, New Hampshire, and Lexington, Kentucky, until retiring to Maine in 1994. He writes from a liberal Jewish perspective that may not always reflect a traditional understanding of some aspects of Judaism.

★   ★   ★

We were roommates at Dartmouth College for three years in the late 1940s and early 1950s and have been corresponding on a regular basis ever since. In recent years our correspondence turned to the subject of our respective religions. In the course of our letters, each of us realized that he knew relatively little about the religion of the other, and that what we thought we knew was often wrong or confused. Consequently, we agreed to explain some of our basic religious beliefs and ideas to each other in order to clarify points of confusion and difference that were occurring in our correspondence.

Because we have remained close personal friends over the years, no aspect of our religious beliefs or religiously held moral outlooks was considered out of bounds for the give-and-take of this probing and challenging correspondence. Each of us vigorously expounded and defended his religion against the often skeptical comments of the other. In this series of "letters to a roommate," points of difference and similarity, agreement and disagreement, confusion and new insight emerged—often in very sharp focus. We engaged in a one-on-one dialogue that we believe is unique in the history of Jewish-Mormon relations, and we want to share it with others.

As a result of our lengthy correspondence, we came to believe that if the religious differences we had faced were roadblocks to full understanding between two good friends, then even more so would many other Mormons and Jews need help in understanding the practices, tenets, and teachings of these two great world religions, and how the two traditions relate to each other.

It is probably fair to say, however, that Mormons as a group are much more interested in Judaism than Jews are in Mormonism. This is partly because Mormons actively proselytize non-Mormons, including Jews, and partly because the Mormon library of sacred literature includes the Hebrew Bible, the fundamental Scripture of Judaism, as well as the Christian New Testament, the Book of Mormon, the Books of Abraham and Moses, and the

Doctrine and Covenants, all of which refer in some degree to the Jewish people. However, because Mormons know about Judaism primarily from Scripture, they encounter great difficulty in dialogue with present-day Jews. Modern Judaism is far different from what is depicted in the Bible.

Mormon interest in Judaism is further reinforced by the fact that Mormons consider themselves to be part of the House of Israel, both ancient and modern. Jews find this belief very confusing and reject the idea of a connection between the two religions. Nonetheless, that connection is the basis for the title of our book.

For all of these reasons, we think that Mormons, with their scriptural emphasis, need to know more about Judaism, and especially postbiblical Judaism. And Jews need to know more about Mormonism in order to be able to better appreciate why Mormons believe and behave as they do, and why they feel a historical and religious kinship with Jews, and especially why they include Jews in their proselyting efforts.

Because the world is growing smaller, people of different religious backgrounds will be encountering one another more often than in the past and thus will have a more urgent need to understand one another than heretofore. When they come into contact, they may well find that while the world outlooks of their respective religions differ, the differences are based on strong, established traditions and beliefs that make sense in their own context even though their presuppositions may seem quite foreign to those of another background.

Thus, our primary purpose in writing this book is to promote greater interreligious understanding for both Jewish and Mormon readers, as well as to overcome some of the difficulties in communication between the two religions that we discovered during the course of our correspondence (and may still have).

The format of this book is primarily expository. Each of us has written four chapters explaining some of the basic ideas, beliefs, and practices of his religion, noting the similarities and differences between the two faiths as we go along. These chapters are presented in alternating order—first one on Judaism, then one on Mormonism, and so on—and we conclude with a final chapter, written by both of us together, in which we summarize our respective religious positions and list some of the sources of friction and misunderstanding that we have discovered. This concluding chapter is not intended to belittle the tenets and traditions of either religion, for each of us understands that the other finds his own religion appropriate for himself. We hope, however, that this book will stimulate Jewish and Mormon readers to understand and appreciate, though not necessarily agree with, the sources and depth of feelings and the faith with which each religion approaches humanity's relationship with God.

We give you this book which attempts to explain these two religions, one to the other, with candor and openness. We hope that the adherents of each religion will benefit from our efforts, so that understanding, respect, and fellowship between them will be encouraged and increased.

Chapter 1

The Basis and Background of Judaism

Judaism is the religion, or, one might say, the religions, of the Jewish people. We prefer the plural because Judaism has changed greatly over the course of the centuries. One cannot claim to understand present-day Judaism simply because he is familiar with the religious beliefs and practices of the Hebrew Bible (or the Old Testament, as Christianity calls this collection of ancient literature). Similarly, one cannot fully understand organized Christianity today solely because he has read the New Testament, or, more specifically for our purpose, one cannot understand the present structure of the Mormon Church because he has read the Book of Mormon. Both Judaism and Mormonism are far more than their basic literature. They are the end products of their respective histories. Each has grown and matured in its thinking, outlook, and practices since its inception: Judaism from its beginnings in the Pentateuch, and Mormonism since the revelation to Joseph Smith at Palmyra, New York.

Both religions are the products of revelation, each in its own way. Judaism began with God revealing Himself to Abraham and commanding him to leave his home. Isaac, Jacob, and Moses all conversed with God. The biblical prophets expanded on these early revelations, conveying

1

their own revelations from God to the people of their time. The end result is the story of the Children of Israel as recounted in the pages of the Hebrew Bible.

Contrary to what many non-Jews may think, however, Judaism is not primarily biblical. In fact, it is far more postbiblical in nature. Many of its most distinctive features are based upon the Oral Torah, a huge body of interpretations, spiritual insights, and understandings of the many layers and nuances of meaning found in Scripture offered by the rabbis over the centuries. The Oral Torah embodies a sense of ongoing revelation, though in a very different way from what we find in the Written Torah, that is, the Pentateuch. In essence, the Oral Torah is an ever increasing body of Jewish sacred literature that seeks to fathom the multileveled meanings in the Bible and to understand God more fully as He relates to any given situation. According to Jewish tradition, the two Torahs are of one piece, for as Rabbi Dov-Ber Pinson, an Orthodox rabbi, states, "the oral tradition is one with the written, and it is impossible to understand one without the other." The Bible begins with the Five Books of Moses, known in Hebrew as the Torah, or more specifically for our use here, the Written Torah. The word *Torah* does not mean "law", as it is often translated, but rather "teach" or "instruction" and is akin to the Hebrew word for teacher.

In sharp contrast, Mormonism, as understood by Latter-day Saints, is the product of God's revelation to Joseph Smith in 1820 in Palmyra, New York, and the subsequent development of a religion based upon that revelation, as well as subsequent revelations to the leaders of the church since that time. These forms of postbiblical revelation are extremely different, with the Oral Torah comprising centuries of interpretations and insights into the biblical text, and the Mormon one claiming a relatively recent direct link to God.

Akin to the different understandings of what revelation means, and just as important for a sound comparison of the two religions, is an awareness of the fundamental difference in outlook between them. As the reader will see in Mr. Johnson's chapters, he frequently presents a dichotomy of right or wrong, true or false. Mormonism tends to view the world in this fashion. There are few gray areas; very little ambivalence. It is an either/or approach to life's questions and situations. In sharp contrast, Judaism's approach is both/and. We tend to see nuances, options, alternatives in many of life's challenges. As a result, Judaism may well encompass conflicting views on the same subject without feeling a need to accept one and negate the other. For a good illustration of how this approach is implemented in practice in regard to specific, real questions that arise in the course of life, see the rabbinic materials quoted in Appendix 3.

The both/and approach is reflected in the ability of many modernist Jews to accept the Written Torah as pertinent religious teaching, a fundamental element of our religion, and at the same time to recognize that the accounts of events in Genesis and Exodus may not be historically accurate. Modern Jews are not disturbed by the findings of biblical scholars who conclude that the Pentateuch was compiled by different authors and redactors over a period of many centuries and reflect their editing of the events it reports. This approach also permits Judaism to take a situational view of ethical questions, though still maintaining the overarching principle on which they are based. In this respect it is very different from the position presented by Mormon leader Elder William R. Bradford in his October 1999 General Conference address entitled "Righteousness," in which he states, "In every case which confronts us in life there is either a right way or a wrong way to proceed."

With these brief introductory comparisons we turn to the basis and background of Judaism. In the Book of Genesis, the first book of the Pentateuch, or Written Torah, we find the beginnings of monotheism among the Hebrew patriarchs—Abraham, Isaac, and Jacob—unlike Mormonism which has many more patriarchs. God revealed Himself and communicated with the patriarchs in many ways. He first spoke directly with Abraham when he commanded him to leave Ur of the Chaldees and become a blessing to the world. He spoke to him through the voice of an angel in the biblical episode known as the Akedah, the "binding" of Isaac and his near-sacrifice in Genesis 22. He communicated through dreams in the account of Jacob's ladder and in the stories of the dreams that Joseph interpreted to his brothers and to Pharaoh. Worship took place at high places or at altars that the patriarchs built for their animal sacrifices. There was no functioning intermediary priesthood in the religion of Genesis in either the Aaronite or the Melchizedek tradition, nor were there any words associated with the sacrifices that resemble what we call prayer today. What we read was primarily in the nature of bargains: "If you, God, will do such-and-such, then I will . . ." There were no holidays to observe. There were no ethical command-ments or ritual acts to be fulfilled, although Abraham is certainly aware of appropriate ethical behavior when he argues with God prior to the destruction of Sodom and Gomorrah. The religion of this period is quite straightfor-ward and basic. In essence, it is the rather simple religion of a family (Abraham, Isaac, Jacob and his children) grop-ing to know a God who has called them from among all other families and singled them out to serve Him alone.

In Exodus, the second book of the Bible, Judaism began to develop from the religion of a family into the religion of a larger group, the Jewish people. This people, under the leadership of Moses, left the slavery they had known in Egypt and began forty years of wandering in the Wilderness of Sinai. The seminal event of this period was their encounter with God at Mount Sinai, where they experienced a theophany, a profound revelation from God. They made a covenant (the Hebrew word is *b'rit*), a bargain, even a contract, with God, specifying that they would be His people and He would be their God, con-tinuing the covenant made with Abraham. They received the Ten Commandments, as well as other laws and statutes that were intended to govern their corporate life. Exodus contains the first references to the Sabbath (aside from the creation story at the beginning of Genesis) and to the five major Jewish holidays: Pesach (Passover), Shavuot (Pentecost), Rosh Hashanah (New Year; though only later called by this name; in Exodus it is the Day of the Horn Blast), Yom Kippur (the Day of Atonement), and Sukkot

(Booths or Tabernacles). Jews still celebrate all of these holidays, although in ways far different from what the biblical text describes.

The Book of Exodus, then, recounts the beginning of Judaism as the religion of the Jewish people, who became a religiously distinct people in the pages of history, and have continued to worship their God until this very day, although in ways far different from what we find in Exodus.

Whether the books of Exodus and Genesis are factual accounts of the events they report is of lesser importance to us as a people of faith than the spiritual insights and lessons they convey. Reflective of our both/and outlook, the non-traditionalist Jew is able to accommodate in his understanding of the Bible both modern scholarship, which questions the historical accuracy of its narratives, as well as the Oral Torah tradition, which provides us with a means of understanding its religious lessons. The modernist Jew does not bring his secular understanding of the text to his religious understanding of it. For the traditionalist modern biblical scholarship is not a concern.

The remaining three books of the Torah—Leviticus, Numbers, and Deuteronomy—deal with the establishment of a priestly class known as Kohanim (the descendants of Aaron, not of Melchizedek) as well as its helper tribe, the Levites. These books also describe the building of the Tabernacle as a place of worship and look forward to a Temple to be built at some future time, in which the priests and Levites are to officiate at ritual sacrifices. The Sabbath and the five holidays are further discussed, some in much greater detail than others. There are many laws directed at both personal and communal behavior, teaching ethical and ritual principles intended to guide the people in every aspect of their lives. These books contain the rudiments of a formalized religion that was further expanded upon and developed by the biblical prophets and even more so by rabbis, sages, and teachers from biblical times until the present.

As mentioned above, many Jews today, especially non-traditionalists, view the Torah, not as literally accurate history, but as religious literature incorporating historical narratives, legends, laws, ethics, and accounts of Judaism's beginnings, a literature that tells us of our early ongoing relationship with God. While many traditionalist Jews (a term we will discuss below) may accept the biblical account of creation, the stories of the patriarchs, or the Exodus saga as actual historical events, their emphasis, too, is far more focused on the religious lessons and spiritual insights to be learned from these narratives through the Oral Torah than on spending time verifying their accuracy. The modernist Jew is not concerned about the historical accuracy of these accounts. He can view them as a product of their time and place without specifying which parts are the product of human editing and which are historically accurate. As the Bible is open to many different modern scholarly theories as to its origins, the religious lessons found in the text take precedence. And while there are Jewish biblical archaeologists among the scholars searching the ancient ruins of Israel today, there is no institution in Judaism devoted to verifying the historical accuracy of the biblical record.

In contrast, the Foundation for Ancient Research and Mormon Studies does attempt to establish the historical plausibility of the Mormon Scriptures. This kind of academic investigation to verify the biblical accounts and the beginnings of our religion is not a primary Jewish concern in the same way. Here then is another difference that Mormons encounter when they try to understand Judaism. Substantiating the historical accuracy of the text (not just the first two books, but all of Scripture) is not the focus of our concern; rather it is the religious lessons and spiritual insights we can garner from the text that merit our attention, as illustrated in the passage from the rabbinic interpretation of Psalm 9 quoted in Appendix 2.

Judaism utilizes the original Hebrew language of the Torah to study and understand Scripture. Some Hebrew words have more than one meaning or do not translate very well into English, as was noted above in regard to the word *torah*. Therefore, the Mormon concern for the biblical text "as far as it is translated correctly" is meaningless for Jews.

Since many Hebrew words have more than one meaning, especially key words pertaining to important theological and ritual concepts, there cannot be a single "correct" translation. This is no problem for Jewish readers of the Bible, however, for taken together the several possible renderings of any term in English enhance and enrich our understanding of what the original Hebrew Scripture is telling us. Furthermore, Jewish tradition, the Oral Torah, posits that there are special insights, teachings, and truths that go far beyond what is apparent in the literal text. These are embodied in the specific words of any given passage of the Torah. They can be discovered if one analyzes such matters as the specific grammatical form in any given passage (e.g., plural vs. singular, masculine vs. feminine, one tense instead of another), or the choice of a particular word instead of some synonym. Even the shapes of the individual letters or how something is spelled where there is more than one possible spelling, as well as any ideas suggested by puns, wordplays, or homonyms can provide insights. If the Torah were in English rather than Hebrew, for example, Jewish expositors might seek to find the relation between *red* and *read* if both appeared in the same passage, or, say, between *mouse* as an animal and as a computer tool; again, see Appendix 2 for some illustrations. These are all vectors to an understanding of God and what He expects of us as His children created in His spiritual image, that is His moral and emotional attributes, and not in His physical image, as Mormonism posits.

Every generation of Jews has searched through the text of the Hebrew Bible, its words and its letters, seeking an ever-increasing meaning within them. This provides Judaism with a way of interpreting the Bible through the Oral Torah, going far more intensely into the nuances of meaning found in the texts of these five books as well as all the other books of Scripture, far beyond the literal words themselves.

The idea of the Oral Torah, as indicated earlier, is based on the rabbinic teaching that God gave Moses two Torahs at Mount Sinai. One was written down: the Pentateuch, the outer layer of God's revelation. The second layer of revelation, transmitted orally to Moses and thus called the Oral Torah, contains all the countless insights and interpretations that can be found in the written text, as well as the means of comprehending them to the fullest. These are the inner layers of the text. In our effort to understand the biblical text, our religious knowledge and understanding continue to increase. Oral Torah becomes a form of ongoing revelation (very different from what Mormonism knows as revelation) and is the basis for Judaism's vast literary heritage dealing with ideas and behavior, in essence extending revelation into each succeeding generation.

Before considering the Oral Torah in greater detail, we need to stop for a moment and discuss revelation as we find it in the prophetic books of Scripture. Since the first century B.C.E.,[1] Judaism has held that this form of revelation, that is, God speaking directly to a prophet who then transmits the message to the people, ceased in the time of Ezra. Ever since, as far as Judaism is concerned, there have been no more prophets in the biblical sense. Thus, from the Jewish standpoint, neither Jesus nor Joseph Smith, nor anyone else, can be considered a prophet.

Why the rabbis declared that prophecy had ended in the time of Ezra is not clear; neither the Bible nor the rabbinic literature spells out their reasoning. However, judging from some of the apocryphal works from the period between the end of the Hebrew Bible and the writing of the New Testament, the decision was probably impelled by the appearance of many men calling themselves prophets during the dark days of the Syrian and Roman

---

[1] C.E., standing for "common era," that is, the calendrical era shared in common with others, is the preferred usage among Jews for A.D., which is deemed inappropriate because of its implicit Christian message as the abbreviation for the Latin *anno Domini*, meaning "in the year of the Lord." B.C.E., meaning "before the common era," is the counterpart of B.C., "before Christ."

persecutions, prophets with very different and often conflicting messages.

We do not know who made the decision, nor exactly
where or when. What we do know is that prophecy had
become a babble of tongues, and from then on there was
to be no more revelation in Judaism in the classical sense,
nor would Judaism accept the revelations of other religions. The accepted method of religious insight, from
then on, was the Oral Torah, a totally new form of revelation. In it the rabbis often spoke of communicating
directly with God, not in the earlier prophetic fashion, but
through study, discussion, and interpretation of the biblical text, which to them was God's word.

The Pharisees, genuine innovators in Judaism who
were, unfortunately and inaccurately, maligned in the
pages of the New Testament, developed this method of
biblical interpretation sometime in the first century
before the birth of Jesus. The New Testament uses it
freely, quoting the Hebrew Bible to support points it
wishes to make. In modern times this is known as the
proof-texting methodology; that is, one cites a proof-text
in the Bible to establish an idea. Both Judaism and
Christianity continue to use this method, each in its own
way, to support their scripturally based beliefs (for a
glimpse at how the method functioned in the ancient
rabbinic literature, see Appendix 2).

The eighth chapter of this book will serve, among
other things, as an illustration of proof-texting at work, as
used by Mormonism to derive from the Bible and from
its own sacred literature its claim to affinity with ancient
Israel and modern Judaism. This method brings together
different texts to present a specific idea not necessarily

found in full in any one of them. Mr. Johnson, in accord with his religious heritage, uses it to convince the reader of the truth of the Mormon message, an approach which Jews find highly conversionist in nature.

We can now return to our consideration of Scripture. The Judaism of the Torah developed more fully in the remainder of the Bible. The literary prophets—Isaiah, Jeremiah, Amos, Hosea, and the others—spoke at length about ethical issues and the type of behavior that was acceptable or not acceptable to God, both for the individual and for the Jewish people as a whole. King Solomon built a Temple in Jerusalem in which proper worship was to occur, with the Aaronite priesthood (not the Melchizedek), assisted by the Levites, officiating at the sacrificial services, and strong injunctions by some of the prophets against worshiping at other sites. Many of the Psalms appear to have been used in the Temple worship as prayers and hymns, speaking to God and about God in beautiful poetic language.

Other biblical works help us to further understand the nature of God: Jonah conveys a sense of God's concern for all humanity; Job tries to answer the question of why there is evil; Proverbs speaks to human understanding and wisdom; Lamentations mourns the destruction of Jerusalem; Ruth not only describes the love between a woman and her mother-in-law, but is also the earliest record of an individual converting to Judaism. And there is much more.

The Hebrew Bible then, as a whole, is primarily a book about the Jewish people and its growing relationship with God, recounting both its achievements and its failings. While the Bible came to have universal appeal, with both Christianity and Islam holding it in great esteem and regarding it as foundational to their respective faiths, historically its primary focus continues to be the Jewish people.

But Judaism did not cease developing with the Bible, as we have already indicated. A couple of centuries after the time of Ezra (ca. 400 B.C.E.), a group of religious teachers, about whose origins we know very little, came to the fore and moved Judaism well beyond its biblical roots. This group, known as the Pharisees, used the Oral Torah to add many new spiritual insights, ideas, and practices to Judaism by juxtaposing passages from different sections of the Bible. Pulling together and quoting biblical texts, they enhanced Judaism's spiritual life. They developed the belief in an afterlife, which is not directly mentioned in the Bible, with its hope of a reward for the righteous and punishment for the wicked. But as Sheol in the Bible, they did not spell out the details of the afterlife, unlike the emphasis given it in Mormonism.

The Pharisees understood that God need not be worshiped solely with sacrifices in the Temple in Jerusalem, but that acceptable worship could also occur with words in an alternative place of worship, called a synagogue. This place of worship is not mentioned even once in the Bible. It appears to have developed some time after the period of the Maccabees (about 150 B.C.E.) as it is not mentioned in either of the books of Maccabees found in the Apocrypha. However, the synagogue was so well developed by the time of the birth of Jesus that it was found throughout the Jewish world of his time. The New Testament tells us that both Jesus and Paul regularly frequented synagogues. Its pattern of worship, using words rather than sacrificial rituals, became the model for church worship with prayers, hymns, sermons, and Bible readings.

The Pharisees fleshed out the rudimentary observance of the Sabbath and the holidays found in the Torah. They developed special rituals that symbolically conveyed the spiritual and historical meaning of the Sabbath and holidays: the blessings welcoming the Sabbath and the ritual of the Passover Seder, to name but a couple. They taught ethical maxims and applied them to life's situations. They began to develop an elaborate code of moral and ritual commandments, known as Halachah—a Hebrew word related to the verb meaning "walk" or "go," and best understood as the "way" in which one ought to go, that is, conduct oneself, both ethically and ritually. The Halachah eventually came to direct every detail of the life of an observant Jew from the moment he awoke in the morning until the time he retired at night.

In subsequent years, as the Jews were dispersed to many different countries, the philosophical currents of the cultures in which they lived had an impact on Jewish thought. Perhaps the best illustration of this tendency was the philosopher Moses Maimonides, who was born in Spain and lived in Egypt in the latter part of the twelfth century. Maimonides book is the *Guide of the Perplexed*, attempts to synthesize Jewish thought with the neo-Aristotelian philosophy of the Middle Ages. Over the centuries there have been countless other rabbis whose teachings and writings have had a significant impact on Judaism. In addition, poets have added beautiful words to the synagogue worship and to Jewish literature. Teachers have embellished the observance of holidays.

As time passed and conditions changed, Jewish communities often faced new and confusing problems that required answers in accordance with the Halachah. They directed such questions to leading rabbis known for their sagacious judgment and knowledge of the Halachah. These rabbinic decisors would respond with thoughtful analyses and recommendations, known as responsa, based upon thorough research in the vast library of halachic writings that had accumulated over the centuries, ever trying to increase the individual Jew's understanding of what was proper religious behavior in every situation in life. The responsa process is still going on in our own day, for questions requiring religious guidance continually come up in the real world. As even a casual perusal of the responsa will show (see, for example, the two examples included in Appendix 3), these questions at first glance appear to be as much secular as religious, for to Judaism, every aspect of life is religious; nothing is outside the scope of religious concern or judgment.

Judaism also has a mystical aspect, known as the Kabbalah (sometimes spelled Cabala). Jewish mystics believe that the Torah is the word of God in its every word, every letter, and even the way in which the letters are written on the Torah scroll. Consequently there must be hidden meanings in all of these forms. The mystical tradition searches the Torah to seek out insights and messages that the ordinary person will not see, often comparing how the same word is written in different passages, unusual usages of words, unusual spellings, and in many other ways constantly seeking to bring the individual Jew closer to God through a deeper appreciation of the Torah in its every facet.

One of the favorite methods of the mystics utilizes the numerical values of Hebrew words. This approach, known as gematria, is based on the fact that the letters of the Hebrew alphabet are also numbers, so that every word in the Torah has a numerical value that can be calculated by adding up the values of the letters comprising it. The mystics believe that there are profound relationships, conveying hidden meanings, between seemingly unrelated words, phrases, or sentences that have the same numerical value.

The mystics also applied their way of comprehending God's word to Jewish rituals, adding greater sanctity of meaning to their observances. They developed an elaborate symbolism for God's celestial kingdom, attempting to understand Him better and to draw ever closer to Him. Throughout Jewish history mysticism has existed alongside the more rationalistic manifestations of Judaism, though not always amicably. It has conveyed its spiritual understanding of God and human life to Jews who would attune themselves to its deepest mysteries.

In modern times, as a living religion, Judaism has continued to develop. Traditional Judaism (also known as Orthodoxy) has consolidated the rituals and many of the ideas of the past into very set ways. Modernist Jews (members of Reform, Conservative and Reconstructionist denominations) have attempted to reformulate many of the rituals and ideas for our time, the aim being to retain those which appear to be relevant and appropriate for modern life, while laying aside those which seem to have lost their relevance.

Unlike Christianity, though, the distinctions between the traditionalist and modernist approaches are more often focused on matters of ritual behavior than on the niceties of theological debate and belief. Moreover, the changes made by the modernists are not "writ in stone." Thus today's non-traditionalists are reevaluating rituals and ideas that were discarded a century ago, and many of these have come back into practice and belief. Judaism, as the "religions" of a living people, functions in this way, which can surely be confusing to Mormons.

Judaism has changed greatly since the time of the Bible, always with the intent of adapting to the challenges it has encountered over the centuries. It will no doubt continue to change as it meets the challenges of the future. The Jewish religion is the ongoing product of the covenant that Abraham made with God so long ago, and which the entire people renewed at the foot of Mount Sinai.

The covenant brought with it for the Jewish people a collective acceptance of a special relationship of service to God, one which has been maintained over the centuries. We express it regularly in both word and deed. We express it in the blessing recited before the reading of the Torah in the synagogue, when we declare that God "has chosen us from all peoples and given us His Torah." We state it in the ritual circumcision ceremony of each male infant on the eighth day after birth. This ceremony, known as B'rit Milah, the Covenant of Circumcision, is a time when we joyfully welcome a newborn child into the family of Israel, praying that his future will be one of religious study, a happy and blessed marriage, and a life filled with deeds of loving kindness.

A sense of religious purpose as well as historical continuity, in a way that Mormonism does not know with its emphasis on freedom of choice in religion, is a part of the everyday life of the observant Jew, who is expected to fulfill countless mitzvot (ritual and ethical obligations) and to praise God regularly for this privilege as he performs them.

Judaism is a religion that encompasses all of life. This understanding is best epitomized by the injunction in Leviticus 19, where God commands the Children of Israel to be holy as He is holy. In fact, this is the very purpose of Judaism: to sanctify life, to add a sense of holiness to everything we do, from the most mundane to the most sacred. The numerous ethical injunctions found in this chapter of the Torah are a précis of how a Jewish person is expected to behave in order to sanctify his life, perhaps best compacted in the words found in verse 18: "You shall love your neighbor as yourself: I am the Lord."

Through our awareness of this teaching, and many others, we bring holiness into our daily actions. In Judaism ethics is integral to religion and the religious life. No human action can be excluded from religious scrutiny.

To assist us in retaining this awareness, Jews recite many blessings aimed at reminding us of God's presence in our lives in everything we do—from waking in the morning, to tasting a new fruit, to performing our bodily functions, to fulfilling the ritual commandments. All of these blessings, begin with the phrase "Blessed are you, O Eternal our God, Ruler of the Universe," words reflective of our intimate relationship with God, as indicated by the use of the word "you." This introductory formula is followed either by a reference to the situation we are acknowledging or, when it comes to an activity, whether ritual or otherwise, in which we are about to engage, with the additional words, "who has sanctified us with His mitzvot and commanded that we do such-and-such"—whatever it is for which we are reciting the blessing.

Jews view themselves as having covenanted with God to sanctify all of life. This obligation occurs in every life situation. It is reflected in our words of prayer, not just in the synagogue but throughout the entire day. It makes Judaism a religion primarily of doing rather than of believing. Thus Judaism is far more than a "faith" in the usual English, Christian usage of the word. Rather, it is a religion in a much broader sense: one that encompasses an ancient and historic people, that sees all human behavior as open to God's judgment, with a rich tradition of beliefs and practices. For us, doing is the way we show our faith.

Chapter 2

The Basis and Background of Mormonism

In this chapter I will give an overview of Mormonism. My object is to show the Jewish reader some basic similarities and differences between traditional Christianity and Mormonism. In addition, the Mormon concepts of truth, prophets, restoration, and revelation will be outlined, and an introduction to the prophet Joseph Smith, the Book of Mormon, "covenant people," and modern-day Mormonism will be provided.

Mormonism is best understood through the word "restoration." At first glance, Mormonism may appear to be yet another Protestant religion that was formed in response to concerns that existing Christian denominations had strayed from fundamental Old and New Testament teachings about the Messiah and His gospel. However, Mormonism's unique response to this problem is that the return to God's pure doctrines came about in the early 1800s through the direct intervention of God the Father and His Son the Christ. Members of the Church of Jesus Christ of Latter-day Saints (also referred to as the Mormon Church or LDS Church) believe that an interactive relationship has existed between God and man starting with the first prophet of this "dispensation," Joseph Smith. The Mormon Church is based and founded upon the reality of direct, modern revelation from God in the classic biblical meaning of that word. Through the calling of "latter-day" prophets, and under the direction of God the Father, Mormons affirm that Jesus Christ, the Son of God, has once more *restored* to the earth the fullness of His true gospel and church, both of which had been altered or lost over the intervening centuries following the death of the original apostles. And in a very real sense for Mormons, Jesus Christ Himself stands at the head of this restored church.

As with Judaism, so too one can refer to Christianity in the plural rather than the singular, for it too has passed through changes and transformations since its origin in the first century A.D. The so-called orthodox Christianity came into being in the fourth century and was generally defined by the Council of Nicaea in 325 A.D., with subsequent elaborations and creedal statements by other church councils. However, there developed over time a very broad spectrum of Christian belief, practice, and scriptural interpretation. This led to major doctrinal disputes, apostasies, and schisms within the Christian world, and sometimes to fratricidal conflict, such as the Wars of Religion following upon the Protestant Reformation. Less-deadly conflicts have continued even up to the present day. This is one reason why the Restoration became necessary.

For Latter-day Saints the Restoration is the answer to the problem of the centuries-old Christian confusion over belief and practice. This is what makes Mormonism not just another Christian denomination, but quintessentially Christian. Mormonism claims to be the custodian of God's restored plan of eternal progression for His children. This claim, at best, makes Mormonism unique in modern Christianity (and at worst the object of intense resentment from other "brands" of Christianity).

"True" and "truth" are words that we Latter-day Saints take very seriously and that relate to concepts in which we believe absolutely. In contrast, Jews have great difficulty with these words when applied to religious concepts and teachings. They became immediate stumbling blocks to understanding between Rabbi Leffler and myself in our correspondence. What is true for a Mormon would not necessarily be true for a Jew, not only because of their different religious and cultural traditions but because the very word "true" has a different meaning in a Jewish religious context. Mormons believe in absolute truth, whether it be scriptural, ethical, or moral, and most Jews do not. We say, for example, that the Book of Mormon is true, meaning that it is historically and religiously accurate, or that the church is true, meaning that its foundation and doctrines were and are divinely inspired. This is an ongoing problem inherent in any Mormon-Jewish dialogue. It is among the most basic of the differences that members of the two religions encounter when they seek to understand one another.

Mormons believe in certain divinely revealed truths that do not change with social mores or philosophical fashions. Some of these truths are discussed in later chapters. However, that which is divinely revealed does not necessarily lend itself to absolute verification by any form of intellectual study, scientific method, or man-originated philosophy, which we sometimes refer to as the "wisdom of men." Mormons honor, respect, and encourage learning and scholarship, but we also recognize the limitations of these disciplines in the area of ultimate religious knowledge, the kind that moves us from within and connects us to God in a personal way. We understand that *eternal* truths from God come only by means of God-given revelation, through ancient and modern prophets duly called and authorized by God to speak the mind and will of deity. Each individual can then know, for himself or herself, by means of a spiritual confirmation, or testimony, that what these prophet/revelators speak and write is from God. These truths and this spiritual confirmation constitute the rock upon which Mormonism rests.

Although this is a significant difference in emphasis and approach between Mormonism and modern Judaism, there are also some significant similarities between Mormonism and *ancient* Judaism. Each religion is based upon direct revelation from God through prophets, whom the ancient Jews recognized and accepted as such. Just as the development of Judaism from the religion of a family to that of a people begins with the encounter with God at Mount Sinai, Mormonism also begins with a theophany, the appearance of God the Father and Jesus Christ the Son, as separate beings, to the boy Joseph Smith near Palmyra, New York, in the spring of 1820. This appearance came to him in response to his prayer that he might know which of the contending churches in his area was true. In the course of this appearance, one of the two beings pointed to the other and said to Joseph, "This is my beloved Son, hear Him." God the Son then informed the fourteen-year-old boy that he had a mission to perform, and that details of the mission would be forthcoming. Mormons refer to this initial experience as the "First Vision." It is the opening event of the Restoration. By means of subsequent angelic visitations and the conveyance by them of the proper authority, God then reestablished a priesthood to the earth that is authorized to act in His name.

Just as Moses was called as a prophet on a mission to lead his people out of Egypt and to communicate to them the mind and will of the Lord, so was Joseph Smith called by God as a prophet in order to restore a fractured, diluted, and partially deceived Christianity to its original purity as established by Christ and His apostles. Like Moses, Joseph Smith became a great leader of those who accepted him as a prophet. Through Joseph Smith, God gave a whole series of revelations, upon which the Church of Jesus Christ of Latter-day Saints was founded and organized in similar fashion to the original Christian Church. For example, its sixth and seventh Articles of Faith state: "We believe in the same organization that existed in the Primitive Church, namely apostles, prophets, pastors, teachers, evangelists and so forth. We believe in the gift of tongues, prophecy, revelation, visions, healing, interpretations of tongues, and so forth."

Both Judaism and Mormonism are based upon a historical/religious drama. In the case of Judaism, the text for this drama is recorded in the Hebrew Bible—the Christian Old Testament. Mormons believe the Bible, both the Old and New Testaments, to be the word of God. We rely on the Bible. We prefer the King James Version (KJV) as a fundamental Scripture, and study it regularly in our search to understand God and His expectations for us.

This said, however, one of the most curious and distinguishing features of Mormonism is our use of a companion scriptural tome to the Bible: the Book of Mormon. This book, known as the keystone of our religion is, like the Bible, both a secular and a religious history. Chronologically, it overlaps portions of the Bible, covering the period from approximately 600 B.C. to 400 A.D. Geographically, its story-line begins in Jerusalem, but most of its text recounts the religious and secular history of a branch of the House of Israel that migrated to the New World, in the region of present-day Central America.

Before elaborating on the content of the Book of Mormon, however, I should explain the link between this ancient text and Joseph Smith.

Three years after his First Vision, Joseph had a second heavenly manifestation. In his own words:

On the evening of the 21st of September, 1823, while I was praying to God, and endeavoring to exercise faith in the precious promises of Scripture, a sudden light like that of day, only of a far purer and more glorious appearance and brightness, burst into the room, indeed the first sight was as though the house was filled with consuming fire; the appearance produced a shock that affected the whole body; in a moment a personage stood before me surrounded with a glory yet greater than that with which I was already surrounded. This messenger proclaimed himself to be an angel of God, sent to bring the joyful tidings that the covenant which God had made with ancient Israel was at hand to be fulfilled. . . . I was informed that I was chosen to be an instrument in the hands of God to bring about some of His purposes in this glorious dispensation.[1]

This resurrected being then informed young Joseph that "there was a book deposited, written upon gold plates, giving an account of the former inhabitants of this continent, and the source from which they sprang." He also said that "the fullness of the everlasting Gospel was contained in it, as delivered by the Savior to the ancient inhabitants."[2]

The messenger, whose name was Moroni, told Joseph that the plates were buried on a hillside near Joseph's

---

[1]Joseph Smith, *History of the Church of Jesus Christ of Latter-day Saints*, volume 4, pp. 536, 537.
[2]Ibid., volume 1, p. 12.

home. Moroni, who had lived on the American continent around 400 A.D., had written a portion of the book himself, and had buried the record shortly before his death. The record is the history of certain "former inhabitants" of the Americas, written by their prophet leaders, and contains the fullness (meaning completeness) of the Gospel of Jesus Christ, the Messiah. It includes an account of the appearance of the Messiah to these people in the Americas shortly after His crucifixion and resurrection in Jerusalem. In recognition of his key role in the Restoration, a statue of Moroni appears on the highest point of many Mormon temples.

Joseph Smith translated this record through the power of God. It has come to be known as the Book of Mormon, called that because the editor and compiler of most of the record, the author of part of it, and the father of Moroni, was a prophet general named Mormon. Just before Mormon was killed in a final battle that virtually annihilated his people, he entrusted the records to his son, Moroni. After escaping from the battle area and wandering for nearly forty years, Moroni buried the plates on which the records were written, and these were delivered nearly fourteen hundred years later to the boy prophet Joseph Smith. This text, used by Mormons as a companion Scripture to the Bible, is therefore the source of the nickname "Mormons" and "Mormon Church," an understandably shorter and easier label than the official name, The Church of Jesus Christ of Latter-day Saints.

The Book of Mormon is mainly a compilation of the records of a group of Jews and the people with whom they probably intermixed after their arrival in the Americas. They and their descendants on the American continent kept these records from 600 B.C. until 421 A.D. The Book of Mormon also contains a much briefer history of an earlier people, known as the Jaredites, who came to the Americas from the region of the Tower of Babel about 2000 B.C. and flourished here until approximately 400–200 B.C.

The main story-line of the Book of Mormon begins in Jerusalem about 600 B.C., when a prophet named Lehi is warned in a dream to flee from the city with his family in order to escape the impending Babylonian conquest. Together with another family they traverse the Arabian wilderness to the coast of what is probably modern-day Oman. They build a ship there and make their way across the Pacific Ocean to the Western Hemisphere.

After Lehi's death in the New World, the families break up into contending factions; the more righteous are led by a younger son named Nephi, while those who rebel against Nephi and his group are headed by Lehi's oldest son, Laman. Much of the Book of Mormon is devoted to the frequent warfare between the two groups, who become known as Nephites and Lamanites. The record climaxes, first, with an appearance of the Messiah, Jesus Christ, to the Book of Mormon peoples in the Western Hemisphere, and finally, 350 years later, with a great battle between Nephites and Lamanites near a hill called Cumorah, in which the Nephites are virtually destroyed. One of the few Nephite survivors, the aforementioned Moroni, then adds his historical notes and religious testimony to the records compiled by his father, Mormon, and buries them, acting under the direction, protection, and foreknowledge of God, to await the time when they would be brought forth to the world by the young prophet Joseph Smith in the latter days preceding the Second Coming of Jesus Christ to the earth.

In his introduction to the record (frontispiece), Mormon wrote, in part,

> Wherefore, it is an abridgement of the record of the people of Nephi, and also of the Lamanites—Written to the Lamanites, who are a remnant of the house of Israel; and also to Jew and Gentile . . . Which is to show unto the remnant of the House of Israel what great things the Lord has done for their fathers; and that they may know the covenants of the Lord, that they are not cast off forever.—And also to the convincing of the Jew and Gentile that Jesus is the Christ, the Eternal God, manifesting himself unto all nations.

Latter-day Saints take the Book of Mormon to be a literal history of real people who lived in a real place in a real time. Mormons, no less than Jews, focus primarily on the religious insights and messages of their Scriptures. Nonetheless, the historical accuracy of the Book of Mormon is important to us in our missionary work because it is the most tangible evidence to a non-Mormon that Joseph Smith was an authentic prophet of God.

The source material given to Joseph Smith by Moroni was written in a lost language known as Reformed Egyptian, which we surmise was an economical shorthand for Hebrew. Joseph Smith had only a limited basic education, let alone any exposure to other languages. Furthermore, Reformed Egyptian is a language not known at the time, so it is illogical that he could have had any outside help. Therefore, Joseph could not have translated it except by a divine power not his own. From a logical perspective, we make the point that if the Book of Mormon itself is authentic, then Joseph Smith was an authentic prophet of God, and therefore the church that he founded through modern revelation is also authentic as a modern-day guide for God's children.

The critics of the Church of Jesus Christ of Latter-day Saints well understand the logic of the above proposition. They come mostly from the ranks of fellow Christians who do not accept modern revelation or believe that God would again call prophets on the earth. And because of the uniqueness of the Book of Mormon in Christianity, and because it is such a tangible reminder of Mormonism's fundamental claims, they devote much time and effort trying to prove that the Book of Mormon *cannot* be historically accurate and that Joseph Smith, therefore, was a false prophet.

Admittedly, there is no absolute scientific evidence that confirms the historical authenticity of the Book of Mormon. Likewise, neither scientists nor secular historians have successfully confirmed the Exodus or many other events described in the Hebrew Bible. Nevertheless, the lack of empirical evidence does not seem to have discouraged either Mormons or Jews from believing deeply in the religious teachings of the Hebrew Bible, and in the case of Mormons, of the Book of Mormon as well.

However, there is a noteworthy difference between Jews and Mormons over the relevance of the historical accuracy of their religious books. As Rabbi Leffler indicates in the preceding chapter, Jews in general regard the Hebrew Bible primarily as religious history rather than literal history. Many modernist Jews are not concerned with the historical accuracy of either Genesis or Exodus. On the other hand, almost all Mormons, like most traditionalist Jews, take it for granted that the Pentateuch (Written Torah) is historically authentic. Mormons also take it for granted that the Book of Mormon is true (meaning that it is historically authentic and contains religious truths).

However, we do not base our faith upon, or expect, incontrovertible proof of the accuracy of the text. We understand that God does not prove anything to His children in this manner, although He may provide evidences as a support for faith. Faith, by definition, rests upon a belief in things that cannot be empirically demonstrated. Thus, a Latter-day Saint's testimony of the Book of Mormon, and of Joseph Smith as a prophet, typically comes from study and prayer and then a spiritual witness of these truths rather than through the application of the socratic or scientific method.

A spiritual witness or "testimony" is essentially a *feeling* for truth. Such a feeling is difficult to explain or describe to someone who has not experienced it. In the

Mormon Church, we sometimes characterize it as a "burning in the bosom" that is communicated to one's spirit-self rather than to one's physical mind or intellect. It is a form of personal revelation that transcends unaided, purely human reason. We consider that this witness comes to us through the Holy Ghost, the third member of the Godhead.

Nonetheless, possession of such a witness does not require Mormons to be totally uninterested in scientific discoveries that may support their faith. Therefore, many Latter-day Saints, including a large number of Mormon scholars who devote full time to the subject and are associated with the Foundation for Ancient Research and Mormon Studies, follow new discoveries regarding Mesoamerica (Central America and southern Mexico) with great interest. We are gratified that many of the most recent archaeological and other discoveries and conclusions tend to support the historical accuracy of the Book of Mormon record.

The Church of Jesus Christ of Latter-day Saints officially takes no position on who the Book of Mormon peoples were or where they lived, only that it was somewhere in the Americas. The church specifically does not claim that the Book of Mormon is the history of all the native peoples of the Western Hemisphere. However, almost all Mormon scholars now believe that Lehi landed on the coast of Central America, where other peoples were also present, and that the Jaredite and Nephite/Lamanite civilizations were, respectively, the Olmec and preclassic Mayan civilizations.

This conviction is based upon internal evidence from the Book of Mormon and external evidence from archaeological findings since the Book of Mormon was published. The geographical clues given by the multiple prophet-writers strongly suggest a setting in and around the Isthmus of Tehuantepec in southern Mexico and Guatemala. The many ruined cities discovered in this area since the publication of the Book of Mormon in 1829 lend further credence to this view. The carbon-14 method of dating ancient ruins places the time period of the Olmecs and early Mayans in close proximity to the Book of Mormon dates. In this connection we always point out that Mormon scholars seek only to demonstrate historical *plausibility*, not absolute proof. We believe that the Book of Mormon is itself the best evidence for its authenticity.

Regardless of what particular foundation a Mormon's or a Jew's faith is based upon, both religions respect and revere the writings of their prophets.

Mormons and Jews share another, more modern, heritage: persecution and intolerance. In the case of the Church of Jesus Christ of Latter-day Saints, the basic problem has been, and still is to a very large extent, the refusal of fellow Christians to accept our belief that God would call modern prophets and give modern revelations (even if they concede that God could do this if He chose to, they insist that He did not do so in the case of Joseph Smith and Mormonism). This is at the heart of what differentiates Mormonism from all other Christian churches. Of course it is also an important difference with Judaism.

We should point out, too, that while Mormons accept without reservation the teachings of the New Testament, we do not accept the postbiblical creeds, such as those developed at Nicaea and Chalcedon (451 A.D.), which have been adopted by much of orthodox Christianity, but which we regard as unbiblical *interpretation* of Scripture. Based upon modern revelation, Mormon doctrine also includes certain concepts that are not specifically included in the Bible, but do not contradict it. Among these are its beliefs regarding the premortal and postmortal state of the human family, as will be explained later. This also has led to much opposition from fellow Christians.

In the early days of the Mormon Church, this opposition was often violent. Most historians would agree that no other religious group in America has been so hated, despised, and vilified as the Mormons because of their beliefs and practices. Following the establishment of the church in Fayette, New York, on April 6, 1830, hostility toward it began almost immediately. Largely in response to this opposition, and, we believe, as guided by God through Joseph Smith, church members moved to Kirtland, Ohio, in 1831. From there they were commanded by the Lord to "gather" to Missouri, where, in the late 1830s, they became victims of mob violence so severe that many were murdered in cold blood.

This opposition was stirred up in part by hostile Christian ministers and in part by earlier settlers of Missouri who feared that the Mormons were becoming a political threat. The governor of Missouri at one point issued an order threatening the Mormons with extermination if they did not leave the state. Joseph Smith and some of his associates were arrested and thrown into prison; the Saints (as the members of the church were called) were driven from their homes by lawless mobs, and their property was stolen. They found a temporary refuge on the banks of the Mississippi River in Illinois and built a beautiful city called Nauvoo, then the largest city in the state.

The persecution resumed. In 1844, Joseph Smith and his brother Hyrum were brutally murdered by a mob while under arrest in jail at Carthage, Illinois, supposedly under the protection of the governor of Illinois. Following this traumatic event, the Saints were forced out of Nauvoo in 1846 and literally expelled at gunpoint from what was then the United States, once more by hostile mobs.

An American exodus then occurred, similar in some respects to the Hebrew exodus from Egypt. Under the leadership of their new prophet, Brigham Young, the "American Moses," the Saints made one of the great pioneer treks in American history. Hundreds died crossing the plains to the Mormon promised land—the Salt Lake valley in Utah, where the first group arrived in the summer of 1847. Many others followed and began to settle throughout the Great Basin, once again temporarily free from their enemies.

Even there, however, they continued to be harassed, especially by territorial judges and justices after Utah became a territory in 1850. Eventually, after the Mormons renounced their practice of limited plural marriage in 1890, Utah was admitted as a state in 1896. Following the so-called Smoot Hearings of 1903–07 in the United States Senate, Senator-elect Reed Smoot from Utah, who was also an apostle and a senior leader of the church, was allowed to take his seat, and legal discrimination ended.

Today, Mormons are highly respected and much better understood by most people. Church members occupy high positions, such as cabinet officers, members of Congress, ambassadors, admirals and generals, and captains of industry. The Mormon Church is no longer a Utah church or even an American church, but is well established in most of the countries of the world. A majority of its nearly eleven million members now live outside of the United States.

Latter-day Saints have always felt a particular affinity for Jews and for other members of the House of Israel. We consider ourselves to be literal, or adopted through baptism, descendants of the twelve tribes of Israel. This lineage is revealed to us in our patriarchal blessings (as will be explained in chapter 8). There is much in the Book of Mormon concerning the latter-day "gathering" of Israel; for example, 3 Nephi 20:29:

> And I will remember the covenant which I have made with my people; and I have covenanted with them that I would gather them together in mine own due time, that I would give unto them again the land of their fathers for their inheritance,

which is the land of Jerusalem, which is the promised land unto them forever, saith the Father.

One of the early Mormon apostles, Orson Hyde, journeyed to the Holy Land in 1841, where, on October 24 of that year, on the Mount of Olives, he prayed to "dedicate and consecrate this land for the gathering together of Judah's scattered remnants" (for the full text of his prayer, see Appendix 1). Brigham Young University has established a Jerusalem Center for Near Eastern Studies on the Mount of Olives, with the approval and blessing of the Israeli government, if not necessarily of the Orthodox Jewish community there. Relations with Israeli Jews have been quite satisfactory since the opening of the center in 1987. In the spirit of accommodation, the university agreed with the government of Israel that the center would be used exclusively for educational and cultural activities. There would be no proselyting of Israeli Jews, even outside of Israel. That agreement has been scrupulously kept.

The members of the Church of Jesus Christ of Latter-day Saints, like the Jews, consider themselves to be a covenant people, both collectively and individually. In the sacred history of the earth, covenants were made with Adam and Eve and with all the ancient patriarchs and prophets and their wives—from Adam down to Moses at Mount Sinai. Today, at baptism, and in their temple ordinances, Mormons also make sacred covenants with God. They see these covenants as modern counterparts of the covenants made in biblical times. Members who are faithful to the promises they make will receive great blessings. If they violate their covenants, they must expect that these blessings will be denied them.

Mormonism is a revealed religion, and its hierarchical organization reflects this premise. At the top, acting always under the inspiration and direction of the Lord, there is the First Presidency, consisting of the president of the church and his two counselors, and the Quorum of the Twelve, consisting of twelve apostles. The president is considered to be the prophet for the whole church, and is the presiding high priest, but all of the men in the First Presidency and the Quorum of the Twelve are esteemed as prophets, seers, and revelators in their own right. Below them there are five other quorums of "general authorities," called Seventies. Most of these men serve full-time in overall leadership positions in the church throughout the world. They may receive living expenses if necessary, but in most cases they have already achieved financial independence from their secular careers.

The local congregational units of the church are known as "wards" and "branches." The local units are presided over by a bishop or branch president and his two counselors, and are organized into "stakes," which also have a president and two counselors at their head. There are typically between five and ten wards in a stake. The word "stake" comes from Isaiah 33:20, which refers to the stakes of Zion. The leaders of these organizational groups are "called," or assigned, to these positions by those in authority above them. The callings are based upon inspiration from the Lord. Everyone who serves in the church is a volunteer. There is no paid ministry in the Church of Jesus Christ of Latter-day Saints.

Because church members generally assume that the designation of their hierarchical leaders is done prayerfully and involves inspiration from God, there is very strong membership support for the church's organizational structure as well as for its basic doctrines and beliefs. There is also great respect for the words and counsel of its leaders, especially when they speak in their capacity as prophets, seers, and revelators. Moreover, as will be discussed in chapter 6, the church is a closely knit social organization that strives to fulfill or support the temporal, as well as spiritual, needs of its members.

It should be apparent from the preceding brief description that the Church of Jesus Christ of Latter-day Saints is not just another Protestant church. It stands alone, not only within Christianity, but among other religions and religious institutions, in its assertion that it is led by a prophet of God. No other religion bases itself upon *direct, modern, continuing* revelation from God, as Mormons do in a very literal sense. As will be explained later, these claims strongly influence the church's emphasis on missionary activity. They are the basis for its existence and for the message it proclaims to the world.

Chapter 3

Jewish Religious Ideas

Most Jews are born into Judaism. The sole requirement is to have one Jewish parent. Until modern times this was exclusively the mother. Nowadays, in some branches of Judaism, it is sufficient to be the child of a Jewish father.

On the other hand, there are many people today who convert to Judaism. This usually occurs after a lengthy period of study culminating with certain rituals, such as going to the mikveh (ritual bath) for both men and women, ritual circumcision for men, agreement to maintain the Sabbath and dietary laws (in the traditionalist branches of Judaism), and usually a conversion ceremony in a synagogue setting. Significantly, these rituals do not include a creedal affirmation that marks the convert's passage from being a non-Jew to being a Jew and becoming a part of the Jewish people in the totality of his or her religious life.

The lack of a creed is worth noting, for it is not what a person believes in any creedal or affirming sense that makes him a Jew, unlike what is entailed in becoming a Christian, and more especially a Mormon. In Judaism the beliefs a person holds come after he affirms that he is a part of the Jewish people, not in the process of getting in, as occurs in Christianity, and therefore in Mormonism. This difference may be especially difficult for Mormons to comprehend because they are so faith-centered. Mormons, in effect, come into the Mormon religion because they accept and share its beliefs and doctrines.

In contrast, Jews first share a common religious history, a sense of all having been present at Mount Sinai and having received the Torah, plus the sweep of Jewish history with its literature, its teachings, and its events, that brings them together as a religious people. For this reason we do not feel any need for theological agreement in order to be considered Jewish. We tend not to ask one another, "What do you believe?" That is a Christian question, which Mormons ask of themselves and of one another, as do members of most other Christian groups, as a way of ascertaining the acceptable beliefs of those who label themselves as Christians. Such a question is not part of the "test" of whether a person is a Jew. As indicated in the first chapter, belief for us would be more correctly seen through actions, rather than any kind of doctrinal statement. To be a Jew is to be part of the historic Jewish people and not of some other religion, and to evidence this by the way in which one lives.

Consequently there is no formalized set of beliefs that all Jews will or must hold and must affirm in some public way in order to be Jewish. However, the lack of defined belief does not mean that there are no central Jewish religious ideas. There are myriads. Rather it means that conformity of belief is not a part of Judaism or of being a Jew. Thus if one were to ask, "What do Jews believe about such-and-such?", there would be no single answer, no dogma, accepted by all Jews.

Judaism, unlike Christianity and certainly Mormonism, does not function in this way. To expect it to do so is to place a non-Jewish presupposition upon it, which unfortunately Christians all too frequently do, an error that to a large degree impedes their understanding of Judaism. Nonetheless, there are many distinctively Jewish teachings and religious ideas. Within these parameters each individual Jew is free to select the ideas that he finds most comfortable and most relevant to his life. And, again unlike the situation in many Christian denominations, including Mormonism, there is no central authority in Judaism to define acceptable beliefs.

Akin to the lack of specificity of belief, Jews do not define, but talk about. We do not spell out the details of Jewish ideas and beliefs. We talk about them, often differing among ourselves. This is in marked contrast with Mormonism, which tends to be very specific about its beliefs and is very concerned about defining them for its adherents.

Judaism's tendency not to define is evident in many different areas. For instance, the Hebrew word *ehad* is usually translated as "one," but it can have a number of other meanings. When we recite it as part of our worship service, we do not do so in a creedal fashion, but rather as a statement of relationship. Likewise the soul and most aspects of the afterlife are not defined, although they too are talked about.

As a consequence, we encounter a problem at the very outset of our consideration of Jewish ideas. Where Mormons want clear-cut concepts, with thoroughly defined terms and beliefs, Judaism refuses to provide them, since that is not how we function. Furthermore, we understand that human language is limited and can provide us with only a limited understanding of an infinite God. Thus we continue seeking to comprehend Him through the Oral Torah.

As a result, Mormons are apt to find Jewish religious thought imprecise, whereas their own religious ideas are very clearly and definitively stated. This occurs not because Judaism is intentionally vague, but because Jewish religious ideas tend to be situational, used when applicable and set aside for another time when not. This situationalism reflects the fact, already mentioned, that it is not what one believes or does not believe that brings him into Judaism. This is very much in contrast with the Mormon (and generally Christian) approach.

However, as broad and nondefining as the parameters of Jewish religious ideas are, there are limits. In modern times, the most obvious limit is the acceptance of the beliefs or basic tenets of another religion, that is, the acceptance of Jesus as the Messiah or of Allah as God, primarily because by accepting such tenets the individual and his family begin to function within the orbit of the other religion; within a generation or two they no longer feel a part of the Jewish people (denying the Jews' covenant with God, as we shall discuss shortly), and, more appropriately for them, become part of another religious tradition. Excluding these limitations, each individual Jew is free to select the ideas with which he is most comfortable and which he finds most relevant to his life.

One of the best ways to view Jewish religious ideas is through the words of the Jewish liturgy, the "order" of worship as found in the Siddur, the Jewish prayer book used in the synagogue, which is the proper name for the Jewish house of worship. This institution that came into existence sometime after the time of Ezra and prior to the time of Jesus, and after the destruction of the Temple in Jerusalem in 70 C.E. replaced its sacrificial form of worship. It is the prototype of the church as the place of worship in Christianity, using words to worship—prayers, songs, Bible readings, and sermons. People pray for what is important to them. They pray for what they believe matters (even if others may not agree). Thus the words of the liturgy are a good place to begin our search for Jewish religious ideas.

Perhaps most central to Judaism from an historical standpoint is the affirmation of God as *ehad*. The words come from Deuteronomy 6:4, "Hear, O Israel, the Eternal is our God, the Eternal is *ehad*," and are recited morning and evening in the synagogue.

This affirmation is considered the cornerstone of Jewish belief, and appropriately so. The verse is known in

Hebrew by its first word, *Sh'ma*—"hear." It gives its name to the first group of blessings found in the daily morning and evening worship, however, it is not a creedal statement. It is an affirmation of God as a relationship. God is our God. We have known Him from Sinai until today. How each individual worshiper understands God is a personal matter. One Jew is not about to tell or ask another. It does not matter, since the specifics of belief do not bring the worshiper into Judaism or keep him out.

And *ehad*. The word is usually translated as "one," as mentioned above, but it could mean unique, alone, only, unified or any other understanding of this Hebrew word that comes to the worshiper's awareness as he affirms the relationship. The individual is free to let his interpretation roam to include the vastness of meaning in the Hebrew text.

Even with such a specifically monotheistic view of God, Judaism feels a need to go beyond this declaration. Over the centuries we have developed a panoply of designations for God, words that speak of the many facets of understanding that are part of our awareness of Him. We use such terms as *Adonai,* literally, "My Lord," and a substitute for the biblical YHVH; *Tzur,* meaning "rock"; the biblical words *Elohim,* and *Eloha,* meaning "God"; *Shaddai,* meaning "power"; *Shechinah,* which designates the indwelling presence of God in human life and unlike the other terms is in the feminine form; *Hakadosh Baruch Hu,* "the Holy One, blessed be He" (see the example in the midrashic passage in Appendix 2); *HaShem* (literally "the name", a term that denotes God's otherness and our inability to fully comprehend His vastness); *Avinu Malkenu*, "Our Father, Our King"; *Harachaman*, the "Merciful One"; *Dayan Ha'emet*, the "Righteous Judge"; and on and on.

These alternative divine names make it possible for us to understand God differently in different situations, thereby making God meaningful in every given time and place in the manner most appropriate to it. For example, He is "Our Father, Our King" when, in the liturgy for the New Year and the Day of Atonement, we speak of the conduct He expects of us, but He is the "Righteous Judge" when we learn that someone has died.

Despite His many names, God remains one for us, with no human form, not a God of flesh and bone, not corporeal but purely spirit—in distinct contrast with Mormonism. The divine names satisfy our need for as many ways as possible to comprehend His oneness and how He plays a part in human existence.

The idea of the covenant is another fundamental aspect of Judaism. God made a covenant with Adam and with Noah in Scripture, but the covenant between God and the Jewish people began with Abraham, when God called him from his father's home in Ur of the Chaldees and commanded him to go out and become a blessing to the peoples of the world. This covenant was expanded upon by the ritual of circumcision performed on male infants at the age of eight days and which Abraham performed on himself and his son Isaac. The covenant was renewed at Mount Sinai when the newly freed Israelites stood at its base and proclaimed their loyalty to God by responding, "All that the Lord has spoken we shall do" (Exodus 19:8), and God took them to Himself as a "kingdom of priests and a holy people" (Exodus 19:6).

Being part of the covenanted people, whether by birth or conversion, is a privilege which Jews treasure. Jews view the acceptance of the central tenets of another religion, such as Christianity, as apostasy, a denial of the ancient covenant with God.

Over the centuries the covenant has played an important role both in how Jews view themselves and how other peoples view them. It has been a source of anti-Jewish sentiment when other groups saw Jews as elitist because of their claim to a special relationship with God. However, that was never the intent of the covenant. Rather was it an agreement to serve God (see Deuteronomy 7:6–8), to follow His commandments, both ethical and ritual, even though, as the prophets were wont to point out, the people frequently fell away from doing so.

This relationship is best understood as designed to make it possible for us to sanctify life by the way in which we live. And here again we can return to the pages of the Siddur to gain insight into the intent of the covenant. There are many prayers that reflect this purpose.

One of the most frequently repeated illustrations of the covenantal relationship is found in the words of the blessing that is recited before the reading from the weekly Torah portion in the service, a reading which occurs twice every Sabbath and twice during the week, on Mondays and Thursdays. The pertinent words are: "Blessed are You, O Eternal our God, Ruler of the Universe, who has chosen us from all people and given us His Torah. Blessed are You, O Eternal, Giver of the Torah" (Jewish blessings usually go back and forth between the second- and third-person usages). We are blessing or praising God (the Hebrew word *baruch* contains both meanings) for giving us His teachings, the Torah, that we might know how to live our lives in ways pleasing to Him—that is to say, by doing things pleasing to Him.

The Torah was given to us by a loving God for us "to understand and discern, to mark, learn and teach, to heed, to do and to fulfill in love all the words of instruction in Thy Torah." These words, from the second blessing of the morning, the Sh'ma group of blessings, remind the Jewish worshiper continually of the love relationship that is central to the covenant between God and His people. The blessing continues, "Thou hast chosen us from all peoples and tongues, and hast brought us near to Thy great Name forever in faithfulness, that we might in love give thanks unto Thee and proclaim Thy unity. Blessed art Thou, O Lord, who hast chosen Thy people Israel in love." The Sh'ma itself follows immediately after this prayer.

The covenant, then, is a relationship of love between God and His people. It requires that the people understand, learn, and do God's "statutes of life." Only in this way can the individual Jew sanctify life, that is, be holy, on a daily basis, in order to fulfill his part of the covenant.

This sense of covenant is well reflected in another Jewish prayer, the Kiddush for the Sabbath eve, the blessing over the wine recited (often sung) in the home every Friday evening at the beginning of the Sabbath. It states in part, "For You have chosen us and sanctified us from all peoples." We continually remind ourselves through prayer of this special relationship with God, of this ancient covenant, which we still maintain in the face of centuries of efforts by other religions to make us forsake it, and that its purpose is to make life holy as God is holy.

The Jewish outlook on life is perhaps best epitomized in one of the blessings recited at the ceremony of ritual circumcision, the B'rit Milah (literally, "covenant of circumcision"), usually performed on every male infant on the eighth day after birth (although if there are medical reasons it can be postponed). We pray that as this child grows up, he will be led to Torah, *chupah*, and *ma'asim tovim*: to the study of God's words (Torah), to a worthy and loving marriage (*chupah*), and to do goodly deeds (*ma'asim tovim*). The infant is just beginning his life, and we waste no time in declaring to him (as if he were able to understand) how Judaism expects him to live, for the ceremony of circumcision brings him into his religion as part of the historic Jewish people and thus welcomes him into the covenant established by Abraham so long ago.

Another religious idea found in Judaism is life after death. However, in contrast with traditional Christianity, and especially with Mormonism, it is affirmed but not defined, though over the centuries this belief has played an important role at various times, especially in Jewish mysticism. There are hints of it in the second blessing of the Amidah prayer in the daily service, where we find the following: "Thou sustainest the living with loving kindness, revive the dead with great mercy. . . .Yea, faithful art Thou to revive the dead. Blessed art Thou, O Eternal, who revivest the dead."

This is a reference to the resurrection of the dead, often connected with the coming of the Messiah, but not to an afterlife as the belief is found in traditional Christianity and certainly in Mormonism. However, by implication there is an assumption of a life after death in which these souls have been during the interim period between their death and the coming of the Messiah, when, according to the traditional belief, all deceased Jews will somehow be resurrected and return to Jerusalem. The logistics of this belief are God's concern, but it is the basis of the custom among traditionalist Jews to be buried with a small amount of earth from Israel in the coffin; at the time of the resurrection, so they believe, the holy soil will enable their revived bodies to find the way back to Jerusalem more easily.

In the blessing recited after the reading from the Torah, we find the phrase "who has implanted within us eternal life." This phrase is used in connection with the giving of the Torah, meaning that it blesses us with eternal life, but no further explanation is given.

These few examples are really the only passages in the worship service proper referring to life after death. There

is no description of what goes on or any details of a telestial, terrestrial, or celestial kingdom comparable to what
Mormonism possesses. Judaism has neither the New
Testament nor the Book of Mormon, which are both
major sources of such beliefs. The rabbis of the talmudic
era believed that we should focus on how we live here on
this earth and God will take care of the hereafter. Thus,
while there are many references to life after death in the
religious writings of Judaism, there is no consensus, nor is
it required that one accept any of the teachings about the
afterlife in order to be considered a Jew.

There are also some references to an afterlife outside
of the main part of the worship service. The blessing prior
to the start of the service, which begins with the words,
"O my God, the soul which You gave me is pure," concludes with "Blessed are You, O Eternal, who restores
souls to the dead," a reference more to the immortality of
the soul, that is, the non-physical part of a person (again
not defined), than to life after death.

In addition there is the prayer at the conclusion of the
service known as the Mourner's Kaddish. Even though
this doxology in praise of God has become a memorial
prayer recited in memory of the deceased, its words make
no reference to death or life after death, and the some-
what shorter version of the same prayer recited elsewhere
in the service is not associated with mourning.

Further, in the Jewish funeral service, as well as in any
public memorial service, we find a prayer beginning with
the Hebrew words *El male rachamim*—"O God, full of

compassion." The prayer speaks to our belief that the departed will come into the presence of God and will be "bound up in the bonds of eternal life" and that "his repose [there] will be peace." The hope for eternal life is stated but without any details or specifics. Typically Jewish!

Nonetheless, Jewish tradition speaks of three good places where a person can end up in the afterlife, and one not so good. The three good places are the *Olam Ha-ba* (World to Come), *Gan Ay-den* (Garden of Eden), and *Pardes* (Paradise). The first two terms are used interchangeably, while the third has other connotations as well, but none are defined. What these places are like, other than good, is not spelled out. The best one can find is a statement like: "The righteous of the world inherit the Olam Ha-ba; the wicked inherit Gehenna," this being the not-so-good place, similar to hell in the Christian tradition but again not defined in any way.

The Jewish emphasis is on life in this world, and so, while there are ideas about an afterlife, it is not a focus as it became in Christianity, nor is it described in detail as it is in Mormonism. In part this reflects the Jewish unwillingness to define areas of religious ideas. We may talk about them; we do not spell them out. And in part it occurs because Judaism's emphasis is primarily on how one lives this life; Jews are confident that God will see to it that there are appropriate rewards and punishments in the afterlife without our having to spend time trying to figure out what they will be.

In similar fashion, and again unlike Mormonism, there is no real interest in pre-mortal life, despite the seeming reference to it in Jeremiah 1:5 and a few rabbinic references to this topic. None of these passages has had any major impact on Jewish religious ideas over the centuries.

The Jewish liturgy often refers to God as "Savior." However, the intent of this word is very different from traditional Christian usage and can prove to be a major stumbling block in interreligious dialogue. It does not refer to life after death in any way as it does in Christianity, but focuses on this life. God is frequently referred to in the prayer book as *Mo-shi-ay-nu* ("our Savior") or *Mo-shi-ah* ("Savior"). He is called our "Savior and Shield"; He is "mighty to save" in the second blessing of the Amidah. "There is none like our Savior" are words in a familiar Jewish hymn frequently sung at the conclusion of our worship.

All of these passages, however, refer to God's role in human life, the focus of Jewish concern. It is His love for us as Jews and His giving us His Torah that gives meaning to our existence and "saves" us from leading a base, animal-like existence. The idea of God saving us plays a significant role in Jewish thought, and we reiterate it in worship over and over. But we never use it in reference to a life after this life, as occurs in Christian thought. Here is another significant difference, and one that is often a point of confusion in interreligious dialogue between Jews and Christians.

Similarly, we refer to God as "Redeemer." Once more, this word is not used in the Christian sense of God's saving us from sin in some way. Initially this word referred to God's redeeming us from slavery in Egypt and was connected with the Exodus. Among the verses in the liturgy containing this idea is: "With a new song the redeemed people offered praise unto Thy Name at the sea shore," that is, at the edge of the Red Sea, when He redeemed us from Egyptian servitude. There then follows a passage from the Song of Miriam found in Exodus 15:11, "Who is like You, O Eternal, among the mighty? Who is like You, glorious in holiness, revered in praises, doing wonders?"

In another prayer the word "redeem" refers to our present affliction and oppression. In this prayer we read, "Look upon our affliction and plead our cause, and redeem us speedily for Thy Name's sake; for Thou art a mighty Redeemer. Blessed art Thou, O Lord, the Redeemer of Israel."

Redemption is an ongoing need. It is not redemption from sin, but redemption from oppression, such as the slavery we knew in Egypt, or any other form of human degradation and servitude, conditions still, unfortunately, present throughout the world. The continuing need for redemption is yet another illustration of the Jewish belief that Jesus was not the promised Messiah. Clearly the Messiah is yet to come, since human beings still need redemption from the degradation and oppression of life.

The restoration of Zion, the return of all Jews to Jerusalem, is an important idea in Jewish thought. Until modern times it was always a religious hope, a hope that God, and not human effort, would bring about this miracle, primarily with the coming of the Messiah, at which time all Jews, both living and dead, would be restored to Jerusalem.

In the weekday Amidah there is a prayer for the rebuilding of Jerusalem "speedily and in our days." The Passover Seder concludes with the words, "Next year in Jerusalem," as does the liturgy for the Day of Atonement, Yom Kippur.

These words always referred to a future messianic age when God would reestablish the splendor of the Temple and its worship. In modern times this understanding may be lost to the worshiper because of political Zionism and the establishment of the State of Israel, but its theological intent remains. However, it is problematic whether modernist Jews retain a hope for the restoration of the Temple's sacrificial worship.

Another concern that plays more of a role in traditional Christian thought than in Judaism is sin. This is not because Jews are less prone to sin than others, but because we do not believe in any kind of original sin caused by Adam and Eve. Sin is not a state of being; neither can one "sin in his heart." In Judaism sin is an action. It is primarily related to behavior, not intent. The Hebrew word for "sin" is *cheyt*, originally an archery term meaning "missing the mark," indicating that one's behavior was less than might have been expected, that he had missed the mark in his actions regarding himself, in relation to his fellow human beings, and especially in relation to God.

There were sin offerings in the Temple of old, but the concern for sin did not follow into the worship of the synagogue. *Cheyt* became the focus of the High Holidays, primarily Yom Kippur, in which there is a lengthy litany confessing one's sins, with each instance beginning with the words, "For the sin which we have sinned against You by doing such-and such." The sins named include such human shortcomings as arrogance, disrespect for parents and teachers, gossip, gluttony, sexual immorality, hypocrisy, giving way to our evil impulses, and many more. There is a long list.

On the holy day of Yom Kippur we seek forgiveness from both God and our fellow human beings. But forgiveness can only occur after we have repented of our sinful behavior and determined not to repeat it in the future. Noteworthy also is the belief that God will only forgive us after we have sought forgiveness of those against whom we have sinned. The human relationships have to be mended first. The remainder of the year, Jewish worship focuses much more on mitzvot, on religious responsibilities, on the positive in life rather than on our shortcomings.

There are, of course, many other ideas in the Jewish prayer book, but as with all of the concepts mentioned in this chapter, they are not definitive in nature. They are merely talked about and reflect differing opinions which the worshiper may understand as he finds appropriate and acceptable. Consensus of belief is not required.

Perhaps most telling in this respect is the fact that Maimonides's Thirteen Principles of Faith are found in the additional readings for the daily morning worship service and are not integrally included within it. This positioning is no accident. Rabbi Joseph Hertz, in his commentary on the Thirteen Principles in his annotated translation of the Siddur, wrote:

> Judaism is a system of spiritual truths, moral laws and religious practices. The moral and religious practices have been duly classified, codified and clothed with binding authority. Not so the spiritual doctrines. No formulation of these exists which enjoys universal recognition by the House of Israel. There are various reasons for this. One of them is the fact that Judaism never made salvation dependent upon doctrine *in itself*, apart from its influence on conduct.[1]

As a result, the ideas in the prayer book, as well as all of the religious ideas of Judaism, are always open to discussion, new insights, and even, at times, rejection. This openness and freedom from theological agreement has, in part, contributed to Judaism's being the "religions" of the Jewish people. One does not have to agree in belief in order to be a part of this historic people. Here is an approach to belief and ideas that most religions, and perhaps most especially traditional Christianity and Mormonism, do not know. Consequently their adherents have great difficulty in understanding Judaism. It often

---

[1]Joseph H. Hertz, *The Authorised Daily Prayer Book* (New York: Bloch, 1948), p.248.

appears confusing to them and even chaotic, because they try to force Judaism, the "religions" of a historic people, into the mold of their Christian understanding of what religion entails, which begins with a statement of belief. It does not work!

Chapter 4

The Purpose of Mormonism

As Rabbi Leffler explained in the last chapter, Jews do not define. In sharp contrast, Mormons do define. These definitions are less a theology, which is typically man-originated, than a body of doctrine and truth that has been divinely revealed to modern prophets since the time of Joseph Smith's First Vision in 1820.

The Church of Jesus Christ of Latter-day Saints seeks to help all men and women to live better and happier lives while on the earth, and then to return to the presence of our Heavenly Father when their mortal lives are ended. The purpose of Mormonism is therefore bound closely to the purpose of earth life. That purpose is defined in the context of three basic questions that most people (perhaps even some Jews) ask themselves sooner or later: (1) where did I come from? (2) why am I here? (3) where am I going after death? Speaking through modern-day prophets, God has clarified the answers to these fundamental questions of existence. These answers form the core of Mormon doctrine.

Latter-day Saints accept four books as canonized Scripture. These four "standard works," as they are called, are the Bible (including the Old and New Testaments), the Book of Mormon, the Doctrine and Covenants, and the Pearl of Great Price.

The Doctrine and Covenants is the official compilation of all the recognized and canonized revelations received by prophets of the church since the time of its founding in 1830. Most of these revelations were given through the prophet Joseph Smith, and many of them have to do with details of church organization and practice as it was being established during Joseph Smith's lifetime. Others, however, are major doctrinal revelations that bear upon our pre-mortal and post-mortal existence and our *eternal* potential—meaning what may ultimately become of us.

The Pearl of Great Price contains Joseph Smith's own history of his First Vision and the coming forth of the Book of Mormon. It contains the Book of Moses, Joseph Smith's inspired translation of the biblical Book of Genesis, which clarifies some of the gaps and ambiguities in Genesis regarding the organization of the earth and the creation of man (such as the apparent contradiction between Genesis 1 and 2: the Creation was spiritual before it was physical).

The Pearl of Great Price also includes the Book of Abraham. This book, translated by Joseph Smith from an Egyptian papyrus that came into his possession, consists of a revelation given to Abraham when he was in Egypt. It provides biographical information about Abraham beyond what is given in the Bible and also reveals much more about the order of the universe, the pre-mortal state of the spirit, and the circumstances of a great Council in Heaven, held among the spirit children of God before the earth was created. Like the Book of Moses, the Book of Abraham gives further details about the process of the earth's physical creation.

Here the reader should understand the meanings of "translate" and "translation" as the Church of Jesus Christ of Latter-day Saints uses these words. As mentioned in chapter 2, Joseph Smith was not a scholar. He had little formal education. He did not "translate" the Book of Mormon or the Books of Moses and Abraham as one who knows both languages might translate, say, French into English. He relied upon the power or inspiration of God in order to do so.

The Book of Abraham came into being when rolls of ancient parchment were found attached to one of four Egyptian mummies purchased by the church in 1835. On July 5, 1835, the prophet recorded, "I commenced the translation of some of the characters or hieroglyphics, and much to our joy found that one of the rolls contained the writings of Abraham." Since revelation, and not scholarship, is involved in this type of translation, it is not necessarily of primary importance what the text—in this case the parchment—actually says, but rather the information which the Lord wishes to convey to us.

Joseph Smith also produced an inspired translation of portions of the Bible known as the "Joseph Smith Translation." This contains important clarifications of the biblical text, which we accept "insofar as it is translated correctly"—which may not always be the case. He began the translation in 1830 with an inspired revision of the Book of Genesis, now known as the Book of Moses in the Pearl of Great Price. He continued working on his translation of portions of the New Testament, including the whole of Matthew, chapter 24, for the remainder of his life. He did not go back to the earliest Hebrew and Greek manuscripts to make a new translation into English. Rather, he revised the biblical text by making inspired corrections and additions.

These Scriptures collectively provide the foundation of Mormon doctrine. They provide answers to the questions posed at the beginning of this chapter and illuminate the purpose of earth life. Based upon them, we have the following understanding of this purpose:

Before any of us came to this physical earth, we dwelt as spirit children of our Heavenly Father in a pre-mortal spirit world. Although we had spirit bodies, we were created in the *physical* image of God, and *looked like* our Heavenly parents, as we do now. Although Jews and other Christians interpret the words "image" and "likeness" in Genesis 1:26 as referring only to God's moral and emotional attributes, modern revelation makes it clear that they are to be understood as also reflecting our physical similarity to God. The various anthropomorphic references to God in the Hebrew Bible are in accord with this revelation.

In the spirit world we had friends and associates with

whom we mingled, and we were conscious of the things that were being carried on about us. We realized that in order to follow in the footsteps of our Father it would be necessary to take upon ourselves a physical body. This was the great plan that the Father had in mind for his spirit children. We understood that a place must be prepared where these developments could be accomplished.

The plan for the organization of this planet was formulated and presented to all of us spirit children at the Council in Heaven, where a majority of us voted in favor. We realized that there would be differences of environment, difficulties, and temptations away from the Father's influence that would try mankind, but because of the opportunity of advancement that would result therefrom for those who proved faithful, we voted to accept the plan and take our chances here on earth. Otherwise, we would not be here.

When the spirit is joined with the physical body, a "living soul" results. As we receive our physical, mortal bodies, several other necessary opportunities are opened up to us. We have the opportunity to grow in knowledge and develop our talents and gifts; we will be tried and tested by means of challenges and adversities; we will be given opportunities to carry out those callings or missions to which we were foreordained while still in the spirit world; we are given our "agency," that is, the freedom to make choices for good or for evil; we will have the opportunity to establish an eternal family relationship.

"Foreordination" is the pre-mortal selection of individuals to come forth in mortality at specified times, and under certain conditions, to fulfill designated responsibilities. Abraham, for example, was told that in the pre-existence there were many of "the noble and great ones; And God saw these souls that they were good, and he stood in the midst of them and he said: These will I make my rulers; for he stood among those that were spirits, and he saw that they were good; and he said unto me: Abraham, thou art one of them; thou wast chosen before thou wast born" (Abraham 3:22–23).

A similar instance of foreordination is found in the Hebrew Bible, where the Lord informed the prophet Jeremiah, "Before I formed thee in the belly I knew thee; and . . . I ordained thee a prophet unto the nations" (Jeremiah 1:5).

Foreordination, however, is not predestination. It is the outcome of voluntary choice, not the violation of it. This freedom to make choices, or what the Church of Jesus Christ of Latter-day Saints calls "free (moral) agency," is, or should be unless artificially restrained, the privilege of all human beings.

Mormonism teaches that mortality is thus a dress rehearsal for the next world. That is why we are here.

The spirit's departure from the body at death is often compared to the withdrawal of a hand from a glove. The glove, representing the physical body, is discarded, to be resurrected at a later time, but the hand—that is, the spirit, which is the real "personality"—goes on about its business. Our spirits pass first into the post-mortal spirit world in which the righteous will dwell in a state of happiness known as paradise. The situation of these spirits was revealed in a vision granted to president and prophet Joseph F. Smith (not to be confused with Joseph Smith) on October 3, 1918. In his words:

> . . . the eyes of my understanding were opened and . . . I saw the hosts of the dead, both small and great. And there were gathered together in one place an innumerable company of the spirits of the just, who had been faithful in the testimony of Jesus while they lived in mortality. . . . I beheld that they were filled with joy and gladness, and were rejoicing together because the day of their deliverance was at hand. They were assembled awaiting the advent of the Son of God into the spirit world to declare redemption from the bands of death. . . . While this vast multitude waited and conversed, rejoicing in the hour of their deliverance from the chains of death, the Son of God appeared, declaring liberty to the captives who had been faithful. And there he preached to them the everlasting gospel, the doctrine of the resurrection and the redemption of mankind from the fall, and from individual sins on condition of repentance.
>
> (Doctrine and Covenants 138:11–19)

The less righteous (or "wicked"), however, will be consigned to a "spirit prison." Continuing Joseph F.

Smith's vision:

> But unto the wicked he did not go, and among
> the ungodly and the unrepentant who had defiled
> themselves while in the flesh, his voice was not
> raised. Neither did the rebellious who rejected the
> testimonies and the warnings of the ancient
> prophets behold his presence, nor look upon his
> face. Where these were darkness reigned. But
> among the righteous there was peace.
> (Doctrine and Covenants 138:20–22)

Progression from spirit prison to paradise is possible,
however. Joseph F. Smith's vision further revealed that
Jesus Christ did not personally preach the gospel to the
spirits in prison during the brief period between His crucifixion and resurrection, but rather He organized the
righteous spirits in paradise to do so. Those who accept
their teachings may be liberated from spirit prison.
Ultimately, all spirits will be resurrected and receive once
more their physical bodies in a perfected state. After a final
judgment at the end of the Millennium, those who merit
it will return to the presence of God in His celestial kingdom and become heirs to all that He has. This potentially is where we all can go.

Here, then, is a brief overview of the purpose and plan
of earth life, but some details need to be added, including
a discussion of mankind's ultimate potential beyond this
mortal life.

All of us will commit sins, no matter how earnestly we strive to keep the commandments of our Heavenly Father as they may be reflected in the tenets of mankind's various religions. These sins, however, will be our own. Mormonism, no less than Judaism, rejects the idea of original sin.

Because we will sin, a Plan of Salvation was presented to us at the Council in Heaven. There we agreed and understood that a Savior (in the Christian sense of the word) would be appointed to take our sins upon Himself and pay the price for them. This was necessary because the universe is so organized that mercy may not rob justice. Justice must be served, and the price for sin must be paid.

The Savior appointed was our elder brother, Jesus Christ, known in His pre-mortal existence as Jehovah. Mormons understand that He was the Jehovah of the Hebrew Bible. He stepped forward and volunteered for this role. Under the Father's direction, He created the physical earth. It was He who then came into the world, took upon Himself a mortal body, and through the atonement process, which we cannot fully understand, took our sins upon Himself. He is properly known as the Savior of the World and the Son of God.

Latter-day Saint doctrine sometimes makes a distinction, however, between unconditional and conditional salvation. The first equates with immortality. Immortality is a completely free gift provided to all men and women unconditionally as a result of Christ's death and resurrection. Everyone who ever lived will be resurrected on the earth and will receive again his or her physical body in a perfected, immortal condition—Adolf Hitler no less than Mother Teresa.

On the other hand, conditional or individual salvation—sometimes called exaltation—is something we must earn. This too is made possible in the first place by Christ's death and resurrection (or "grace"), but it is still conditional. The condition is that we must strive to keep God's commandments, and when we stumble, as we sometimes will, that we earnestly repent of our sins and weaknesses.

This is where works come into the picture, and where the Church of Jesus Christ of Latter-day Saints differs from some branches of traditional Christianity. Mormons fully understand and accept the role of grace in salvation/exaltation, but instead of holding that it is by grace *only* that we are saved (i.e., exalted), Mormons cite the prophet Nephi, who wrote in the Book of Mormon, "for we know that it is by grace that we are saved, after all we can do" (2 Nephi 25:23). This implies a life which is not only righteous in a passive way, but also is filled with service to God and one's fellow men, for we are all brothers and sisters. Thus Mormons and Jews are very much alike in that we are both doers.

A few words concerning repentance are in order. Mormons and Jews share this concept as a part of their religious beliefs (see Rabbi Leffler's discussion of sin and repentance in chapter 3). The Mormon understanding of sin is broader than that of Judaism, however. For us, it is quite possible to sin in one's heart. However, the sins of commission are more important. When we sin against our fellow humans, we should express our repentance to them and seek their forgiveness. Minor sins, whether of commission or omission, should be confessed and repented of to our Heavenly Father. Serious moral sins should also be confessed to our bishop and may be the subject of church disciplinary action, designed always to help us to overcome those sins and complete the repentance process (discussed further in chapter 6).

At the time of the Council in Heaven, another of God's sons stepped forward to volunteer his services. This was Lucifer, whose name means "Light Bearer" in Latin and is a translation of the Hebrew *Heylel ben Shakhar*, which means "herald son of dawn" or "morning star." He boasted that he would save every soul by denying man his agency and *forcing* all of the Father's children to obey the Father's law in all things.

Filled with pride, Lucifer demanded God's honor and glory for himself. His plan was rejected, but not until one third of the spirit children had sided with him and were cast out of heaven and down to this earth. Lucifer, otherwise known as Satan after he was cast out, is a real person, who, with his unembodied followers (devils), roams the earth striving to lead men away from the path that will take them back to God.

The belief in Satan as a literal being conditions much of Mormon thought; we refer to him as the Adversary. Satan illustrates the principle of opposition in all things.

Everything in life has its opposite: sickness and health, virtue and vice, joy and sorrow, truth and falsehood, blessings and challenges. It is in the context of these opposites that man is tested and enabled to progress. This progression, potentially, is to godhood itself.

The potential to become gods is understandably controversial outside the church, and needs to be clearly understood. The Church of Jesus Christ of Latter-day Saints affirms that God our Heavenly Father is a *personage*. He is a literal being possessing a physical body of flesh and bone—not blood. A resurrected body, being incorruptible, does not require blood. Blood is a requirement of the mortal condition. He (God) is the preeminent member of the Godhead, which consists of God the Father, Jesus Christ the Son, and the Holy Ghost. The Holy Ghost, through whom spiritual truths are communicated, is a spirit personage without a physical body.

This understanding separates Mormonism from the traditional, post–Council of Nicaea orthodox Christian concept of the Trinity, which Mormons regard as a fundamental error, perpetrated by unbiblical interpretations of what the Bible actually says. Trinitarianism holds that the Father, Son, and Holy Ghost are three persons in one single "essence"—a God "without body, parts, or passions." This concept is overruled for Latter-day Saints by Joseph Smith's First Vision, in which he beheld God and Jesus Christ as two separate personages. For us, consequently, there are three separate beings who together make up the Godhead. They can be said to be *one* God, but one in unity and purpose, rather than one in substance.

Joseph Smith spoke extemporaneously on the subject of our ultimate potential on April 7, 1844, at the funeral of a man named King Follet, and again on June 16, 1844, just before he was murdered. Although his remarks are not formally canonized as revelation, in his King Follet address Joseph Smith said:

> God himself was once as we are now, and is an exalted man, and sits enthroned in yonder heavens! That is the great secret. If the veil were rent today, and the great God who holds this world in its orbit, and who upholds all worlds and all things by his power, was to make himself visible—I say, if you were to see him today, you would see him like a man in form—like yourselves in all the person, image, and very form as a man....These are incomprehensible ideas to some, but they are simple. It is the first principle of the gospel to know for a certainty the character of God, and to know that we may converse with him as one man converses with another, and that he was once a man like us; yea that God himself, the Father of us all, dwelt on an earth, the same as Jesus Christ himself did.

Some say that this makes Mormonism polytheistic. Henotheistic would be a more accurate description. Henotheism is the belief in or worship of one god without denying the existence of others. Joseph Smith explained this in his June 16, 1844, address:

Paul says there are Gods many and Lords many.
I want to set it forth in a plain and simple manner;
but to us there is but one God—that is *pertaining to*
us; and he is in all and through all. . . . I say there
are Gods many and Lords many, but to us only
one, and we are to be in subjection to that one.

These statements put in perspective life's ultimate purpose as Latter-day Saints understand it. For us they make
perfect sense and explain the whole cosmic purpose. The
only God we know of, or whom we worship as God, is
our Heavenly Father, whom we refer to as *Elohim,* the
plural form of the singular noun *'eloah* in the Hebrew
Bible, where it is used 2,570 times as compared to 57
times for the singular. Jesus Christ, the Son of God, is sub-
ordinate to God the Father, but is sometimes referred to
as God in Mormon scriptures because of His role in the
earth's creative process and because of His unity of purpose with His Father.

Moreover, within the vastness of the universe (or uni-
verses) we understand that there are other worlds in the
fifty billions or more of galaxies that are also inhabited by
beings such as ourselves, whose purpose and potential
may be the same as ours, and who may be governed by
gods other than ours. This, however, is purely speculative,
since we have no revelation concerning the governance of
any worlds other than our own.

The seventy-sixth section of the Doctrine and
Covenants is a revelation that was given in the form of a

vision to both Joseph Smith and his associate Sidney Rigdon on February 16, 1832. This vision revealed that there is not just a single heaven as opposed to a single hell, in the afterlife, but gradations to fit the real human condition. The vision detailed the three "degrees of glory" or "kingdoms" to which all those not condemned as "sons of perdition" will be consigned following the resurrection of the physical body and the Final Judgment following the Millennium. Perdition is another name for Satan. Sons of perdition are those in this life who gain a perfect knowledge of the divinity of the gospel, a knowledge that comes only by revelation from the Holy Ghost, and then turn their back upon it and link themselves with Satan in open rebellion against God. This is the unpardonable sin. Their destiny, following their resurrection, is to be cast out with the devil and his angels

Prefacing his record of this vision the prophet wrote:

Upon my return from the Amherst Conference, I resumed the translation of the Scriptures. From sundry revelations which had been received, it was apparent that many important points touching upon the salvation of man had been taken from the Bible, or lost before it was compiled. It appeared self-evident from what truths were left, that if God rewarded everyone according to the deeds done in the body, the term "Heaven," as intended for the Saints' eternal home, must include more kingdoms than one.

Accordingly, while translating St. John's Gospel, myself and Elder Rigdon saw the following vision.

As the two men then testified:

> And we beheld the glory of the Son, on the right hand of the Father, and received of his fulness. . . . For we saw him, even on the right hand of God, and we heard a voice bearing record that he is the only Begotten of the Father—That by him and through him, the worlds are and were created, and the inhabitants thereof are begotten sons and daughters unto God.

For Mormons, this was one of the great, defining revelations. The vision further revealed that the three broad levels in heaven consist of the telestial, terrestrial, and celestial kingdoms in ascending order. Although each is a degree of glory, and therefore desirable, the highest is the celestial kingdom where God and Christ dwell, and the one to which most Latter-day Saints aspire as an eternal home. The requirements for entry are strict, but as will be shown later in the discussion of the role of the temple in Mormonism, this highest kingdom is available to all of God's children, regardless of their mortal circumstances or religious beliefs. The celestial kingdom is sometimes compared with the light of the sun, the terrestrial kingdom to the light of the moon, and the telestial kingdom to the light of the stars.

The only canonized revelation concerning the details of man's potential deification is found in Doctrine and Covenants 132:20–21. Referring to exaltation (in the celestial kingdom) the Lord states:

> Then shall they be gods, because they have no end; therefore shall they be from everlasting to everlasting, because they continue; then shall they be above all, because all things are subject unto them. Then shall they be gods, because they have all power, and the angels are subject unto them. Verily, verily, I say unto you, except ye abide my law ye cannot attain to this glory.

The term "gods" is always used with a small *g*. The King Follet address notwithstanding, most Mormons believe that godhood implies becoming like God the Father, dwelling with Him, and perhaps attaining the power to beget and create, but not full equality with God Himself. There is ambiguity here, and Mormons generally do not worry about the nuances. This element of Mormon belief is discussed more by our opponents than by ourselves.

All of this may naturally be confusing to Jews because they have nothing similar in their tradition. Nonetheless, as any logician would confirm, silence on a subject in one set of Scriptures or traditions does not by itself prove other Scriptures or traditions that speak to the subject to be wrong. Silence proves nothing and therefore is neutral.

Rabbi Leffler mentions that rabbinical commentary posits "three good places in which a person can end up in the afterlife and one not so good." That bears at least a quasi-resemblance to the three degrees of glory and the hell to which sons of perdition are condemned, as given in the revelation to Joseph Smith and Sidney Rigdon.

To reiterate, then, in Judaism the answers to the questions concerning man's post-mortal existence are not defined and of relative unimportance (as are the questions themselves), although very much open to discussion. For Mormons, on the other hand, the questions are front and center, and the answers are of great importance and are spelled out in much more detail by means of modern revelation.

"Families are forever" is a favorite Mormon saying. We believe that the family unit persists beyond the veil that separates the mortal from the eternal condition, and that husbands, wives, and children can be together forever in the post-mortal world. This is why so much emphasis is placed upon building a strong family unity.

Believing as we do that we all have heavenly parents, our highest hope is to be like them. Because of the importance of the family to the eternal plan of happiness, Latter-day Saints believe that Satan makes a major effort to destroy or weaken the sanctity of the family. This is why the church took one of its extremely rare political positions when it opposed passage of the Equal Rights Amendment. The church leaders felt that the amendment would weaken the family relationship.

Women do not hold the priesthood in the Mormon Church. In God's eternal plan for His children, men and women are assigned differing roles. This does not mean, however, that woman's role is regarded as being in any way less important than that of men. The companionship role is the one most often identified for women in the church. Adam "began to till the earth," and "Eve, also, his wife, did labor with him" (Moses 5:1).

This companionship is not limited to the husband-and-wife relationship. The women's organization, the Relief Society, serves cooperatively with the priesthood to carry out the work of the church. Bruce R. McConkie of the Council of the Twelve Apostles emphasized the equality of men and women in things of the spirit:

Where spiritual things are concerned, as pertaining to all gifts of the Spirit, with reference to the receipt of revelation, the gaining of testimonies, and the seeing of visions, in all matters that pertain to godliness and holiness and which are brought to pass as a result of personal righteousness—in all these things men and women stand in the position of ... equality before the Lord.[1]

Church leaders encourage women, when it is possible, to remain in the home as they raise and nurture their chil-

---

[1] *Ensign of the Church of Jesus Christ of Latter-day Saints,* June 1979, p. 61.

dren. This is consistent with the belief that the family should have first priority in all that we do. However, Mormon women also fulfill societal roles, such as physicians, lawyers, professors, administrators, teachers, writers, secretaries, artists, and businesswomen.

In keeping with their understanding of the eternal continuum, Mormons are both this-world and next-world focused. Happiness is the goal for both worlds. The Book of Mormon teaches that "wickedness never was happiness" (Alma 41:10), and Latter-day Saints are urged and taught to keep the commandments of God in all that they do in their temporal as well as their religious lives. Mormonism is thus very similar to Judaism in stressing the interrelationship of religious and secular activities. As one strives to live righteously, he will be blessed in both his mortal and his post-mortal life.

Chapter 5

Jewish Life

Jewish life reflects Judaism as a religion. Because it is a religion that begins with a group of people, Judaism has many facets that reflect patterns of group behavior not commonly considered religious by other religions (Mormonism included) but more akin to an ethnicity. On the other hand, because it is a religion, with worship, ethical concerns, beliefs, and so on, it also has many facets which are spiritual and serve to bring the individual Jew into a personal relationship with God. Both aspects are important. They combine to provide a full, meaningful Jewish existence for the Jew who understands them, appreciates them, and takes advantage of them.

Before we continue with a consideration of Jewish life we must add a note of caution, in order to ensure a more thorough understanding of how Judaism looks at the word "religion." In common English usage this word is usually treated as synonymous with "faith" or "belief." Such usage comes out of Christianity's focus on theology, matters of correct belief, as central to what religion entails. Judaism's understanding of the word "religion" is much broader. It encompasses the Jewish people, behav-

ior, and religious ideas (the latter, of course, include faith
and belief). Thus for Jews, religion has a much broader
meaning than for Christians, and our discussion here will
reflect this greater breadth. The difference in the understanding of what religion involves is crucial for a compre-
hension of Judaism, especially in contrast with
Mormonism.

Judaism is not an authoritarian religion, with a formal,
hierarchical leadership. The structure of Jewish life is
open. It is not defined in a limiting or limited fashion.
Nonetheless, there is a great deal of structure within this
non-defined system, so that the individual Jew may participate and become involved in any number of different
ways, ranging from intensely personal participation at
home, in the synagogue, or in communal organizations, to
almost no participation but a minimalist awareness of
being Jewish. The variations seem almost unlimited and
tend to confuse the Christian, whose choices are far more
restricted, usually defined in some way by an affirmation
of Jesus as the Messiah, church affiliation, and some degree
of involvement in that church. Certainly Mormonism follows this latter pattern.

In looking at a person's Jewish involvement, perhaps
the most meaningful criterion on which to base a judgment is whether the person is or is not a "responsible"
Jew. The choice of the word "good" here would not be
very useful because it so often has primarily an ethical
connotation too limiting to include ritual observances,
although certainly ethical concerns are very much a part

of what being religious is all about in Judaism, as it
assuredly it is in Mormonism. Furthermore, the word
"good" implies its opposite, "bad," which usually has an
ethical connotation, again a difficulty in understanding a
Jewish person's involvement in his religion.

As a result of this Jewish understanding of religion,
one finds a great deal of variation among Jews, both in ritual observance and in participation. This almost laissez-
faire attitude is often a source of confusion to the non-Jew
when he discovers it because he usually lacks an understanding of the Jewish context out of which it comes.

With these brief paragraphs as introduction, we can
now turn our attention to the many facets of Jewish life,
primarily in America, but not overlooking the State of
Israel, for that nation has come to play a significant role in
Judaism since its establishment in 1948.

However, before we proceed, we need to clarify one
more matter: the difference between a traditionalist view
of Judaism and a modernist view of Judaism (I am avoid-
ing the terms "Orthodox," "Conservative," "Reform," and
other organizational designations because they confuse
the issue at this point), for our religion encompasses both
(though not always amicably, as witnessed by the effort of
some ultra-traditionalist rabbis to declare that modernist
Jews are not Jewish).

The traditionalist holds that God, in His revelation at
Mount Sinai, gave two Torahs to Moses and the Jewish
people, one Written, the other Oral, and that it is incum-
bent upon him to follow the Torah and Halachah to the

letter as closely as possible according to the rabbinical interpretations over the centuries. This includes the nuances of the dietary laws, the observances of the Sabbath, the wearing of kosher clothing (which is one-hundred percent of one kind of thread and not a blended fabric), the giving of charity, and many other ritual and ethical laws that govern daily living.

The modernist views Jewish tradition as the product of both God and human understanding, without defining specifically which is which, and in this context he is able to select which ritual aspects of Judaism are meaningful to him, observing those he finds appropriate. He may maintain some of the dietary laws, refrain from doing certain things associated with the workday week on the Sabbath, or not eat leaven during Passover. His observances may well follow many of those of the traditionalist, or they may be very few. However the reason for his choices will be quite different. On the other hand, he tends not to apply this outlook to the ethical lessons of the Torah and sees them as still relevant to his life.

While the distinction between the traditionalist and the modernist is usually theologically based—that is, dependent on how one views the totality of Jewish tradition—the manifestations of it tend to focus not so much on the theological niceties and considerations of an issue as on the ritual behavior they engender.

The purpose of Judaism, as we have mentioned in an earlier chapter, is to sanctify life. This purpose is well illustrated by the life of the individual Jew. In the traditionalist framework, he is expected to say a hundred blessings a day, thanking God for everything he experiences, from the moment he awakens in the morning until he falls asleep at night.

There are blessings for almost every experience in life, and they all reflect our relationship to God and our dependence on Him. Among the more well known are the blessing prior to a meal, the blessing for the Sabbath and holiday candles, the blessing over the wine (called the *Kiddush*, a word which literally means "sanctification"), and the blessing for special occasions. There are also blessings to be recited on seeing lightning, after relieving oneself, before studying Torah, and for almost every other situation.

Some blessings are brief and are merely expressions of appreciation. Others are longer and thank God for the opportunity to sanctify life by doing something, such as eating, observing a holiday, or for a special occasion, such as a birthday or a happy reunion between friends. They all have a specific wording and continually remind the Jew of his dependence upon God for the blessings of life.

Many Jews do not express their religious feelings by reciting blessings regularly in the manner of the traditionalist. Some recite at least some of them more or less frequently, depending on mood and situation, and some seldom, if ever, do so. Nonetheless, blessings are a significant part of the Jewish tradition; they are there to be used and to enhance the Jew's religious life if he so chooses.

The dietary laws are yet another aspect of Jewish life. They are based on passages in the Torah that discuss the permitted and prohibited foods that Jews may or may not eat (see Leviticus 11 and Deuteronomy 14). However, these passages are very terse and with limited detail. They fail to tell us why certain foods are proscribed and not others. Thus we have no basis for assuming, for instance, that they were promulgated for health reasons, even though the coincidence is remarkable. Nor do they go into detail as to how these regulations should be implemented, primarily in the laws dealing with the ritual slaughter of animals or about not mixing meat and milk products at the same meal (the latter based on the statement, "You shall not boil a kid in its mother's milk"; see Exodus 23:19, 34:26, and Deuteronomy 14:21).

Over the centuries the rabbis discussed these regulations as they apply to the religious life of the observant Jew and developed elaborate regulations dealing with them, known as the laws of kashrut—the kosher food laws. And once again we can find traditionalist Jews who will follow these dietary regulations to the letter because they believe that God expects it of them, sometimes even going to extremes. In contrast, other Jews will generally disregard the dietary laws, seeing them as a relic of an ancient aspect of Judaism that has no relevancy for modern life. And in between there are Jews who adhere to these regulations to many differing degrees. Their intent is to sanctify life. Each Jew has the option of choosing to follow these dietary laws or not. A traditional Jew will be more observant; a non-traditional will be less.

Jewish family life involves the celebration of Jewish holidays and rituals not only in the synagogue but also in the home. The most regular holiday is the weekly Sabbath, a word whose basic meaning is "rest," which is what this day is intended to establish. Judaism links the Sabbath to both the seventh day of creation and the Exodus of the ancient Hebrews from Egypt. The Jewish day begins at sundown, reflecting the story of creation, in which each day ends with the phrase "and it was evening and it was morning, one day." As a result the Sabbath begins on Friday at sundown and lasts until Saturday at sundown, Saturday being the seventh day of the week. In the traditional home no work will be done on this day— no kindling of fire (including turning on lights), no cooking, no gardening, and so forth.

The Sabbath is welcomed with special ceremony: the lighting and blessing of the Sabbath candles (usually two to mark the specialness of the day); a blessing, known as the Kiddush, over a cup of wine, whose words specifically tie the Sabbath to both creation and the Exodus; and the enjoying of a special braided loaf of bread known as challah, with its blessing as well. There then follows a special Sabbath meal, prepared to enhance the celebration of this weekly holiday. Again, the traditionalist will enhance the observance of the Sabbath with greater ritual, the non-traditionalist with fewer, but these observances are there to be used and enjoyed, to enhance one's religious life.

As we welcome the Sabbath in the home with special ceremony, so too there is a brief home ritual at the conclusion of the Sabbath called Havdalah. It separates us from the joy of the day of rest and welcomes the workday week once more. This ceremony includes a brief Kiddush, a prayer over a lovely container filled with fragrant spices symbolizing the hope for a pleasant week ahead, and a braided candle reminding us, among other things, of the blessing of fire which only human beings enjoy. The ceremony ends with a song hoping for the coming of the messianic age, of which the Sabbath is considered a foretaste.

The family is also the setting for the celebration of the Passover Seder. There is no comparable ceremony in Christianity. The Seder is a liturgy celebrating the Exodus from Egypt, wrapped around a special meal, with prayers, blessings, songs, questions and answers, an account of the slavery in Egypt of the ancient Hebrews and the deliverance that God brought about, psalms, four cups of wine representing the four promises God made to us—to free us from Egypt, to deliver us from bondage, to redeem us with an outstretched arm, and to take us as His people (Exodus 6:6–7)—and even a game of hide-and-seek to keep the children's attention. There are special foods on the table—matzah (unleavened bread), charoset (a mixture of chopped apple, nuts, and honey) to remind us of the mortar used to build the pyramids, a roasted lamb bone to recall the paschal lamb, maror (bitter herb, most often horseradish, to recall the bitterness of slavery), and other symbolic items. The Seder is an especially joyful occasion celebrated with much anticipation and festivity, and even the most non-traditionalist Jew is apt to be there to participate in the warmth of the family setting.

The home is often the location for the ritual circumcision ceremony of a newborn son on the eighth day, the B'rit Milah, mentioned earlier in this book. It is the occasion for much happiness, welcoming a new life into the household of Israel, reflecting our sense of continuity for the Jewish people and our covenant with God. The ritual is usually performed by a mohel, a person especially trained to perform and officiate at circumcisions. It is followed by a reception in honor of the young child, given by the adoring parents and often grandparents. While historically there was no similar ceremony for girls, a naming ceremony for girls has developed in modern times, though it is more often conducted in the synagogue than in the home.

The family is also the setting for an important part of the rites of mourning. After the funeral the family returns home, and friends and extended family gather round to comfort them. There will be a somber mourning period of up to seven days, with the immediate family members remaining indoors, accepting condolence callers who often bring food so that the family does not have to cook, and who may even take turns in the family's kitchen preparing the food for these days. In addition there is usually a brief memorial worship service in the home in the evening, and often in the morning as well, to comfort the mourners and indicate the concern, caring, and emotional support of the Jewish community for the bereaved.

In these ways, and with the many ritual objects that the family uses to celebrate these occasions and the Jewish

holidays—the Sabbath candlesticks, a Kiddush cup, the
Hanukkah menorah (candelabra), the mezuzah (an orna-
mental box containing a parchment with the words of the
Sh'ma from Deuteronomy 6:4–9) on the doorpost, the
special braided candle and spice box for Havdalah, and
much more—the home plays an important role in Jewish
life. And, as well, there may be works of art depicting different facets of Jewish life: a traditional wedding, Israeli
scenes, rabbis at study, the holidays, scenes from the Bible
or of the lost Jewish world of pre-Holocaust Eastern
Europe.

Equally as significant is the role of the synagogue, the
correct name for the Jewish house of worship. The word
"temple" is also used today, but historically this is incor-
rect, because it properly refers to the building which King
Solomon constructed long ago in Jerusalem and in which
the mode of worship was sacrificial. The word synagogue
literally means "house of assembly" or "house of meeting,"
and as such this institution has served three different purposes over the years: as a place of worship, a place of study
(the Yiddish word for "synagogue" is *shul*, meaning
"school"), and a meeting place for the Jewish community.

First the synagogue is a place of worship. As was discussed in an earlier chapter, Judaism is a liturgical religion
with a set order of worship contained in a prayer book
known as the Siddur. The origins of its liturgy go back
perhaps twenty centuries, and although the prayers have
been enhanced over the years, the general format remains
unchanged.

The Temple in ancient Jerusalem had a daily morning and afternoon sacrificial service. Synagogal worship reflects these services. The Sanctification in the Amidah prayer (mentioned earlier) is complete in both the morning and afternoon worship, but is abbreviated in the evening, when there was no Temple sacrificial service. The Amidah contains nineteen blessings during the week, but only seven on the Sabbath (six regular and a special one for the Sabbath), the remainder being considered petitionary and excluded because the Sabbath is sufficient blessing unto itself. One ought not to petition God for more. The seventh blessing is added on the Sabbath in the middle of the six others. It is a blessing thanking God for the seventh day and its message of rest.

The Sh'ma, mentioned in chapter 3, is recited only in the morning and evening worship. This prayer, with its accompanying blessings, was originally a private prayer, recited upon arising in the morning and going to bed at night. It was brought into the synagogue at an early period to integrate it into the daily worship life of the Jew.

There are blessings, psalms, and other readings prior to the start of the worship service proper to create a prayerful mood. There is a doxology called a Kaddish, usually recited twice in the service, the last time as a mourner's prayer, although it does not mention death. There are hymns and occasionally other inserts into the worship appropriate for special occasions.

Historically, the synagogue was primarily the domain of the male Jew, who was usually able to arrange his schedule to be present at certain prescribed hours of worship. The woman, on the other hand, did not have the responsibility of being present in the synagogue inasmuch as her primary function was in the home, and having to be present in the synagogue at specific times of the day might have conflicted with her family responsibilities. As a result there was a separation of the functioning of the sexes for practical purposes in Jewish life, with the home and synagogue being of equal importance, each in its own way.

The synagogue pattern of worship served as a model for Christian worship. Both contain prayers, Bible readings, songs, and sermons. Thus there is a great deal of similarity between them, although each religion reflects its own religious tradition.

Second, the synagogue serves as a place of study. In the past it was primarily for adult men, though young children might also be present. Today both sexes may be found studying in the synagogue. Judaism is a religion not just of faith but of learning, of study, of knowledge. Historically, Jews have been called the people of the Book, or, perhaps more appropriately, books. Jewish men were expected to be religiously literate. It was not only the rabbis who studied the sacred texts; all men were expected to have some familiarity with them. And the synagogue was the place where such learning took place.

The modern synagogue still reflects this role, and usually has a good-sized school building attached to it for this purpose. Today the classrooms are more often intended for the teaching of young people in a religious school, but they also serve as learning centers for adults. A Jew needs to know what his religion is all about. For us faith requires knowledge, an outlook which is notably different from the basis of faith in Mormonism, which tends to place modern prophetic revelation ahead of intellectual knowledge and academic learning as the primary basis for its faith.

Third, the synagogue is also a meeting place, a center where Jews can get together for many purposes: to socialize with one another, for weddings and wedding receptions, for lectures and musical programs, for funerals and other sad occasions, most any kind of community activity that is appropriate. It has served over the years as a place where the needs of Jews were met: the distribution of food to the needy, and the place where tzedakah ("charity") was distributed. The word *tzedakah* designates charitable giving, but actually it means "justice" or "righteousness," conveying the idea that the help given the poor is on the order of an entitlement to them and not an act of indulgent generosity by the wealthy. Tzedakah, in other words, is a mitzvah, a religious obligation. The synagogue is also the place where strangers and newcomers can go to meet other Jews and share the Sabbath and the holidays with them.

In modern times other institutions have taken their place in Jewish life. Jewish community centers, comparable in many ways to YMCAs and YWCAs, are frequently found in larger urban areas. There are many non-synagogal organizations set up to meet special needs beyond the scope of the synagogue: homes for the aged, fraternal and defense groups, charities, and many more. As the religion of a group of people, Judaism reflects its "peopleness" in many ways not usually found in Christianity.

Holidays play an important role in Jewish life. There are five major holidays, all of which are mentioned up to six times in the Torah. The dates of the holidays are determined by the Jewish lunar/solar calendar, rather than by the civil calendar in general use, and that is why the Jewish holidays appear to occur at different times from year to year.

In the Jewish calendar, which goes back to biblical times, the months depend upon the moon, with each new moon marking the start of a new month. The years are determined by the solar seasons, and so in order to keep the lunar months in line with the solar year we add an extra month every few years, following a set formula for so doing. We also count our years based on the traditional reckoning from creation; thus the year 2000 in the civil calendar is 5760 in the Jewish calendar.

Three of the holidays, Pesach (Passover), Shavuot (Pentecost), and Sukkot (Tabernacles), are referred to as pilgrim festivals because in ancient times all male Jews were expected to make a pilgrimage to the Temple in Jerusalem in order to observe them. The three festivals are connected with the agricultural year as well as with events in biblical history,

Pesach is the first of the Jewish agricultural festivals because it occurs in Nisan, the first month of the Jewish year. It originally marked two things—the harvest of the winter wheat and the spring festival of the shepherds. The account of the first Passover in the Book of Exodus refers to a holiday of matzot (unleavened bread) and a holiday of Passover, seemingly indicating that they originally were separate holidays. However, by the time of the giving of the Torah at Mount Sinai these two festivals seem to have become one, united to commemorate the Exodus from Egypt.

As mentioned above, Pesach's primary celebration is the Seder, often held at the home of the patriarch of the family with all of the family members, and perhaps other guests, gathered around the festive table. The Seder is both a home worship service and a teaching lesson, with the children encouraged to participate so that they can learn the reason for the celebration.

The Haggadah, the book used at the Seder, contains, among other things, questions by four typical children: a wise one, a wicked one, a simple one, and an infant. The wicked son asks, "What mean *ye* by this service?" His question focuses on the Jew's identification with his people, for the response to this query is, "Because he says *ye* and not *we*, he has excluded himself from his people; he would not have been found worthy of participating in the Exodus." In essence he has removed himself, and his descendants by implication, from being Jews. He has denied that he is still part of the covenant with God. He has become an apostate.

Pesach, which lasts seven days for some Jews, and eight days for others, is also a time when Jews eat matzah. During the holiday, not only do we not eat the usual breads and pastry, but also rice, peas, or any other non-leaf or root vegetables that expand when cooked. This limitation is based on the biblical injunction that proscribes eating leaven during the holiday as a memorial of the Exodus and the supposed haste with which it occurred.

Another aspect of the Seder is its hope for the coming of the Messiah, mentioned earlier in this chapter. The prophet Elijah plays a significant role in this message, based on the words found in the last chapter of the book of Malachi: "Behold, I will send you Elijah the prophet before the coming of the great and terrible day of the Lord, and he will turn the hearts of the fathers to the children, and the hearts of the children to the fathers."

There is a special cup for Elijah on the Seder table. It is given a place of honor. In the service after the meal, the youngest person at the table goes to the door and opens it for Elijah while the celebrants welcome him with words of hope. There is also a song expressing the wish for his speedy arrival, a song sung also as part of the Havdalah ritual at the end of the Sabbath, for, as we mentioned earlier, the Sabbath is a foretaste of the messianic age.

The Seder concludes with the words, "Next year in Jerusalem," again expressing a hope for the speedy coming of the Messiah. However, as with so much of Jewish thought, the details of this hope are not delineated in any way.

It is significant that the Haggadah is God-centered. Moses is only mentioned in passing, in a quotation from the Book of Exodus, even though it was he who led the

Children of Israel out of Egypt. The lesson here is that we should not confuse what God did for us when we came out of Egypt with what a human might do. And, of course, that too is a part of the Seder.

The holiday of Shavuot occurs fifty days after the start of Pesach. It originally marked the harvest of the first fruits of the spring harvest. However, it also became linked to the time when the Israelites received the Ten Commandments at Mount Sinai, because the Book of Exodus tells that they arrived at the foot of the mountain in the third month after leaving Egypt, the Jewish month in which Shavuot occurs.

Although the rituals associated with Shavuot are few by comparison with other Jewish holidays, its message is significant. As part of the observance, we read the Book of Ruth in the synagogue because Ruth, as a convert to Judaism, personally accepted the Torah upon herself, just as the Israelites accepted it at Sinai. And in modern times, many congregations have instituted a Confirmation ceremony as part of the holiday observance in which teenagers formally accept their being Jewish after many years of study in religious school, again reflecting an acceptance of Torah for themselves.

Sukkot, the third of the agricultural holidays, occurs in the fall, in the month of Tishri, and marks the conclusion of the growing season in biblical times. It is observed with the building of temporary booths called *sukkot* that are decorated with tree branches and fruits. In ancient times, and even in Israel today, families would take their meals in the *sukkah* (the singular form of *sukkot*) and perhaps dwell in it during the time of the holiday.

Sukkot is also celebrated with the waving of a *lulav*, a palm frond with branches of willow and myrtle attached to it, and the smelling of a fragrant *etrog*, a lemon–like fruit. They are taken up with a special blessing in appreciation of God's bounty.

The conclusion of the eight days of Sukkot is marked by the holiday of Sh'mini Atzeret, an additional joyful observance of the harvest. Added to this observance in rabbinic times was Simchat Torah, the time when we complete the annual reading of the Torah with the final chapter of Deuteronomy and then immediately begin the cycle all over again with the account of creation in Genesis.

Since the Torah holds such a special place for us, this observance is a time of great rejoicing (the name Simchat Torah literally means "rejoicing in the Torah"), with much celebration, singing, and dancing in the synagogue.

In addition to the three pilgrimage festivals, there are two High Holidays, both of which occur in the month of Tishri, the seventh month of the Jewish year, which coincides with September–October on the civil calendar. One of these is Rosh Hashanah, the New Year, though it is not called this in the Torah, but instead is named the Time of the Blowing of the Horn (*shofar* in Hebrew).

Rosh Hashanah falls on the first day of Tishri and begins the Ten Days of Repentance, the most solemn period in the Jewish calendar. It is a synagogue-centered holiday with special prayers and music for the occasion.

The shofar is sounded a number of times during the service as a symbol to arouse the worshiper from moral lethargy and attune him to the need to search his ways and seek forgiveness for his sins of the past year from both his fellow human beings and from God.

At the conclusion of the Ten Days of Repentance is Yom Kippur, the Day of Atonement, the most solemn holiday of the entire Jewish religious calendar. It is a full day of fasting, a holy day with worship services in the synagogue in the evening and throughout the following day until sundown. Its message is one of contrition, repentance, and the forgiveness of our sins. It is a time when we are urged to look at our deeds and measure them against the standards God has set for us. The worship concludes with the sound of the shofar, again calling us to repentance and contrition as we return to our normal everyday lives.

In addition to these five holidays, Judaism also has a number of minor holidays, minor not because they are of lesser importance to us but because their origins are not found in the pages of the Torah.

Probably the best-known of the minor holidays is Hanukkah, which begins on the twenty-fifth of Kislev, which is usually in December. It commemorates the story of the Maccabees, a small group of Jewish zealots who refused to succumb to the enticements of the Greek culture of their time. This story is found in two books in the Apocrypha, dating from about 150 B.C.E.

Led by the Maccabees, the Jews fought against the Syrian king Antiochus who wanted to eradicate Judaism, and they won. After their victory they rededicated the

Temple in Jerusalem (the word Hanukkah means "dedication") and preserved Judaism for the future. Hanukkah is
an eight-day holiday observed with the kindling of candles, one additional on each night, the playing of a game
of put-and-take with a top, and special foods.

Purim is also a minor holiday, based on the Book of
Esther in the Bible. It is a joyous time marking the deliverance of the Jews of Persia from the evil intent of
Haman, the king's prime minister, to destroy them. Queen
Esther is the heroine who saves her people. Purim is celebrated by reading the account in Scripture from a special
scroll called a *Megillah*, with special pastries called haman-
taschen, and lots of joyful noisemaking. It is also a time for
costume parties and giving gifts to the poor.

There are other minor holidays that mark the fall of
Jerusalem to the Babylonians in 586 B.C.E. and to the
Romans in 70 C.E. (by tradition occurring on the same
date, the ninth of Av), the new year of the trees, and other
events in the history of the people.

There are four other aspects of Jewish life that merit
mention in this chapter. One has some similarity to what
is found in Christianity, the other three do not. The first
is Jewish music. In both religions there is music associated with worship, either in a liturgical fashion or expressing beliefs. However, Judaism also has music reflecting the
life of its people—Yiddish lullabies, Ladino love songs (see
below for more on these languages), and modern Israeli
folk songs. Even in modern times Christian music does
not have the breadth of content and kind that Jewish

music has, primarily because it reflects a faith and not a people.

There are several languages associated with Judaism. Hebrew is the primary language of the Bible and the spoken language in the State of Israel. It is also the language of the Mishnah, the first part of the Oral Torah, as will be explained in chapter 8.

Aramaic, a language closely related to Hebrew, was the spoken language of the Near East from shortly before the time of Jesus until the Arab conquest in the seventh century. Several small sections of the Bible are written in Aramaic, and in addition it is the language of the Talmud and much of the Midrash.

Yiddish, a medieval German patois written in Hebrew characters, with accretions of Hebrew and other Eastern European languages, was the language of the Ashkenazic Jews, the branch of Jewry to which the majority of America's Jews belong.

Ladino, a medieval form of Spanish, also written in Hebrew characters with accretions of Hebrew and Mediterranean languages, is the language of the Sephardic Jews, whose ancestors were expelled from Spain in 1492 and settled in North Africa, the Balkans, Turkey, and throughout the Mediterranean region. The first Jewish colonists in North American were mainly Sephardim.

Jewish foodways are also distinct. One can purchase all sorts of Jewish cookbooks, some coming out of the Eastern European communities, others from Mediterranean communities and Israel. Christianity does not have this kind of manifestation. The closest one can come are cookbooks put out by individual churches. In Christendom foodways are generally associated with geography, not religion.

And lastly—humor. There are numerous anthologies of Jewish humor, books that contain humorous stories on almost every aspect of life. Judaism being the religion of a people, its humor covers every facet of the life of this people, frequently self-deprecating, which was a way of living with the oppression which Jews have known over the centuries. Christianity, and certainly Mormonism, knows no comparable literature.

And finally, in this century two salient events have left an indelible mark on the Jewish people.

One of these is the Holocaust, the destruction of the centuries-old Jewish communities of Europe by the Nazis. Starting in the 1930s and continuing until the end of the Second World War in 1945, Hitler planned the extermination of the entire Jewish population of Europe. While some Jews were able to escape, more than six million died in concentration camps during this most barbaric period in human history. There are many memorials to these events, including the Holocaust Museum in Washington, D.C., and lesser museums, parks, and statues in other cities in our country and around the world. We have even established a special day to mark this tragic period in our history, Yom Hashoah, the Holocaust Memorial Day, which occurs in the spring, shortly after the end of Pesach.

The other special event of modern times is the establishment of the independent State of Israel. As mentioned in another place in this book, there are prayers in the Jewish liturgy for the return of the Jews to Zion. However, this was expected to occur with the coming of the Messiah. With the rise of modern nationalism, though, this hope became political in the last part of the nineteenth century. Theodor Herzl founded modern Zionism in 1896. In 1948, after more than half a century of struggle, the State of Israel was proclaimed as an independent nation, to be a haven of refuge for oppressed Jews from around the world.

In the years since, Israel was just that for the ragged survivors of the Holocaust, as well as for Jews who lived in Arab lands and were finding their situation there unbearable. More recently, Israel has accepted Jews wishing to escape from Russia and from Ethiopia.

Israel has also been an emotional focus for the Jews of the Western world, many of whom have visited there to see first-hand the historic sites of the Bible, as well as witness what their co-religionists in that country have accomplished in the half-century or so that it has been in existence. And because Judaism is the religion of a people, when we go to Israel we react with the first-person plural pronoun to what we see: "Look at what *we* have done here," expressing a pride in the accomplishments of our fellow Jews who live there. This is a reaction similar in part to the pride which many Mormons feel in the accomplishments of their pioneer ancestors in Utah.

One other aspect of Judaism that is peculiar to modern times and really has no counterpart in Christianity is
the appearance of secular Jews. These are Jews who are not
religious but have a strong sense of identity with the
Jewish people and Jewish history, which they manifest by
participation in non-synagogal activities, supporting the
State of Israel, and other activities in the Jewish community that are not involved with the synagogue. Peculiarly
there are even some humanist synagogues, whose congre-
gants have excluded God from their understanding of
Judaism but remain strongly identified with the Jewish
people on a non-theological level, and want to show it in
some way. While from a traditional standpoint this is a
truncated understanding of Judaism, nonetheless, because
there is no need for theological agreement within
Judaism, these people do not place themselves outside the
pale.

Judaism offers a rich and varied religious life. Its ways
of doing things are different from those of Mormonism.
Yet it is complete and fulfilling for those who proclaim
themselves to be Jews.

Chapter 6

Mormonism in Practice

Mormons are not born Mormons. They become such either by baptism at the age of eight, which is typical if they are born to Mormon parents, or else they are converted and baptized at a later age. Eight is the age of accountability, as given to the church by revelation (Doctrine and Covenants 68:27), and so baptism is unnecessary prior to that age.

Those who become members of the church after age eight are usually taught a series of six lessons called "discussions." These include our Heavenly Father's plan for His children, the calling of Joseph Smith as a prophet, the Book of Mormon, the Gospel of Jesus Christ, the restoration of the true church, the principle of eternal progression, living a Christlike life, and the responsibilities of membership in the church.

Investigators who would be baptized as new members of the Church of Jesus Christ of Latter-day Saints take upon themselves certain basic commitments. These include tithing of one's income, chastity outside of marriage, and living the "Word of Wisdom."

The Word of Wisdom is a law of health given by revelation from the Lord to Joseph Smith in 1833 (Doctrine
and Covenants 89). It involves abstinence from tea, coffee,
alcohol, and tobacco, and also suggests, among other
things, using meat "sparingly" and eating grains and fruits.
The promise from the Lord in return is, "And all saints
who remember to keep and do these sayings, walking in
obedience to the commandments, shall receive health in
their navel and marrow to their bones" (Doctrine and
Covenants 89:18). We Mormons feel that modern medical science has fully vindicated this revelation.

Those who will not make such commitments are not
baptized.

These are major lifestyle commitments, which most of
the world rejects. Consequently a person generally does
not make them unless he or she first receives some kind
of "testimony"—usually of a spiritual nature, as discussed
in an earlier chapter—that the Book of Mormon and the
latter-day revelations upon which the church is based are
true. It logically follows that all members of the church
who share such testimonies also share a common set of
beliefs and theological tenets. This does not exclude individual differences of opinion, however, on matters that are
not of fundamental doctrinal importance. (Some of these
differences include the location of Book of Mormon peoples, the existence of pre-Adamic men, and the political
role of the church, if any.)

Baptism itself is by total immersion in water and is performed by one holding the priesthood authority to bap-

tize. This includes young men sixteen and older who hold the Aaronic priesthood as well as all holders of the Melchizedek priesthood. In the Mormon Church the priesthood is divided into the lesser, or Aaronic, priesthood, and the higher, or Melchizedek, priesthood (for further details, see the discussion of the priesthood in chapter 8). The Aaronic priesthood is held by all worthy young men from age twelve usually up to age nineteen or so, when they may qualify for the Melchizedek priesthood.

Shortly after receiving the ordinance of baptism, the person baptized is confirmed as a member of the Church of Jesus Christ of Latter-day Saints and given the gift of the Holy Ghost by the laying on of hands. This is done by two or more holders of the Melchizedek priesthood, one of whom acts as voice and adds whatever words of blessing and counsel may come into his mind by inspiration. The gift of the Holy Ghost means the right of the person so receiving it to have the constant companionship of this member of the Godhead as Revelator, Teacher, and Comforter—so long as he or she remains worthy to enjoy it.

Converts to the church now outnumber those born to Latter-day Saint parents because of the rapid worldwide growth of the church. In some respects, new converts have an advantage over those baptized at age eight. Cradle Mormons, as the latter are sometimes known, do not have their testimonies handed to them, as it were, or their religion determined by birth, as in Judaism, but must obtain them in the same way as any other church member, through study and prayer. While it is advantageous to grow up in an active Latter-day Saint family because of early exposure to church practices, standards, and doctrine, this is not a guarantee of later belief and church activity with Mormons any more than it is with Jews. At some point in the maturation process the young Latter-day Saint must discover for himself that the church is true. He must obtain his own spiritual witness. This may come in many different ways, but it often comes through a careful and prayerful reading of the Book of Mormon during the teenage years.

The Church of Jesus Christ of Latter-day Saints has three great missions or purposes for its members: These are (1) proclaim the Gospel of Jesus Christ to "every nation, and kindred, and tongue, and people" (Revelation 14:6), (2) perfect the Saints (i.e., each other), and (3) redeem the dead. All church activities and programs fall under one of these categories.

Missionary work, that is, proclaiming the Gospel to all people, everywhere, is the first great mission of the Church of Jesus Christ of Latter-day Saints. Every member, in fact, is expected to be missionary-minded, whether or not specifically called to that responsibility. "Every Member a Missionary" was the responsibility of each Latter-day Saint proclaimed by President David O. McKay during a solemn assembly held in the Logan, Utah, temple on September 21, 1953.

Christianity, by its very nature, is conversionist. Three times Jesus said to Simon Peter, "Feed my sheep" (John 21:15–17), meaning that His Gospel should be preached to all men: first to the Jews, and then, as was later made clear, to the Gentiles as well.

In the case of Mormonism, the missionary impulse is particularly strong. God does not write in the heavens or appear on CNN News. He has revealed His mind and will through latter-day prophets, and it is through them, and those who follow them, that He expects that the message of the Restoration will be carried to the entire world. From the day of the church's founding, April 6, 1830 (God revealed to Joseph Smith that April 6 was the actual date of Jesus' birth, although we celebrate it on December 25 along with our fellow Christians), Latter-day Saint missionaries have labored diligently to carry out this commandment.

The young men and women who serve full-time in nearly all countries of the world are the most conspicuous Latter-day Saint missionaries. Young men serve for two years and usually begin their missions sometime after their nineteenth birthdays. Young women may go on missions at age twenty-one and serve for eighteen months. Retired couples also may serve full-time missions for either twelve, eighteen, or twenty-four months. Couples are sometimes recruited to specific mission areas by mission presidents who know them personally, but just as often they simply put in their applications and go wherever they are called to serve. Widows may also volunteer to serve missions.

There is no requirement for anyone to serve a mission, and all missionaries do so strictly as volunteers. However, young men are especially encouraged to serve missions.

Besides teaching the Gospel to others and baptizing them into the church, young men, and women also, often benefit enormously from the experience of interacting so closely with others. In the process of teaching, they themselves learn and grow, and their own testimonies of the truthfulness of the Gospel and of the church greatly expand. The missionary field is the foremost training experience for the future leaders of the church.

Jews often find these clean-cut, neatly dressed young men (known as elders) and young women (known as sisters) knocking on their doors. Some may be offended by this proselyting effort, known as tracting, but it might be helpful if they understand the principle behind it.

Because the Gospel of Jesus Christ and the message of the Restoration are intended for all people everywhere, Jew and Gentile alike, efforts are made to offer it to all people everywhere. Tracting is a particularly unproductive form of missionary work because most people, and not only Jews, will reject such an unsolicited approach. Nevertheless, a few people so contacted will be prompted to invite the missionaries into their homes, listen to the discussions, read the Book of Mormon, receive a testimony of its truthfulness and of Joseph Smith as a prophet, and be baptized. These are regarded as the "elect"—perhaps foreordained in the spirit world to hear the Gospel and accept it while in their mortal lives. It is the full-time missionary's responsibility to seek them out, by whatever means prove feasible. A missionary can never know for sure, when he or she knocks on someone's door, what kind of reception awaits. Sometimes, however, elders or sisters may receive a spiritual prompting that directs them to a particular home.

A much more productive missionary effort occurs when members are able to talk to their friends and neighbors about the church, perhaps invite them to attend church services or activities, ascertain some interest, and then invite them into their homes to hear the missionary discussions. This is why every member is a missionary. We Mormons truly believe that we are on to something, and we want to share it with all who will listen.

For some members, missionary work in their own communities is a regular church calling (when one in authority over us, such as our bishop, asks us to assume a church responsibility, we say that we have been "called"— hopefully by inspiration from the Lord—to that position). These are "stake missionaries," who often go out with the younger missionaries during the evenings to teach those who are investigating the church.

Perfecting the Saints is the second mission of the church and is best described by the word "activity." In keeping with our understanding that we must earn our exaltation, we must be "doers of the word" and not merely passive hearers of it. Church members are typically described as "active" or "less active" (which may mean totally inactive). An active Mormon is one who regularly attends church services on Sunday, and who accepts a calling in the church to one of the many responsibilities necessary to the proper functioning of wards and stakes.

Since there is no paid clergy in the Church of Jesus Christ of Latter-day Saints, all such activities are strictly voluntary. The heaviest load typically falls on bishops as a male role and on Relief Society presidents as a female role at the local (ward) level, although each has two counselors and many others to assist him or her in their responsibilities. The bishop is the "father of the ward" and is responsible for the overall spiritual and temporal welfare of his congregation. The Relief Society president ensures that the needs of women, especially, are met. This can include caring for the sick, teaching of homemaking skills, and promoting spiritual progress.

A less active Latter-day Saint is one who attends church meetings infrequently or not at all, and who declines to accept church callings. The reasons vary from a partial or complete loss of testimony to simple apathy. Sometimes the member may succumb to worldly temptations and lifestyle, and feel embarrassed in attending church. The next step in the "falling away" process may be to disparage the church and its leaders. In extreme cases those who leave the church may turn to active opposition. They may become overt anti-Mormons and seek to undermine the faith of others.

Even the most active of Latter-day Saints, however, have no immunity against temptation and human weaknesses. Church programs are designed to encourage the members to help one other to remain faithful and to help those who may be having problems of either a temporal or spiritual nature. The purpose in every case is to help the members to grow and to develop their spirituality, meaning their ability to understand and accept religious truths.

Church services on Sunday run for three separate hours. These may occur in any order, but usually begin with the Sacrament meeting, wherein members partake of bread and water each week and renew their baptismal covenants. The Sacrament meeting is based upon the commandment, "Thou shalt go to the house of prayer and offer up thy sacraments upon my holy day" (Doctrine and Covenants 59:9). The two sacrament prayers, one on the bread and one on the water, are offered by priests, usually young men who hold the lesser, Aaronic priesthood. These two prayers must be said word-perfect and are the only fixed prayers in the worship service. The ordinance of baptism and the temple ordinances must also be pronounced perfectly. Otherwise, all prayers are offered extemporaneously, from the heart. Talks may be assigned by the bishop and his counselors (the "bishopric") to individual members. Those so assigned will thus have the opportunity to speak in church on a spiritual topic. Preparing these talks is one way in which members improve their spiritual knowledge.

The question of spiritual knowledge versus intellectual knowledge, which in Judaism can also be called religious knowledge, came up frequently in the correspondence between Rabbi Leffler and myself. It was a subject of some misunderstanding. For Mormons, spiritual knowledge, of the kind communicated by the Holy Ghost, spirit-to-spirit, is the primary basis for faith, although we are urged to seek knowledge wherever it is to be found, and we are second to none in the importance we attach to education. The excellent quality of Mormon religious scholarship is now ruefully acknowledged even by our opponents.

The contrast here with Judaism would seem to be that Jews tend to emphasize intellectual knowledge per se, coming out of postbiblical rabbinic Judaism (the Oral Torah), as a basis for religious insights, much more than do Mormons. Nevertheless, if the Oral Torah can be said to come from direct communication with God on the part of the rabbis, as Rabbi Leffler states, then this difference in emphasis with Mormonism is much more apparent than real.

The next meeting is usually Sunday School, which is divided into youth and adult classes, all taught by volunteers called to the teaching positions. The Gospel Doctrine class is the primary one for adults, although there is another class called Gospel Essentials for new converts and those investigating the church. The Gospel Doctrine class uses the same lesson format in all chapels throughout the world. Each year one of the four Standard Works is addressed: either the Old Testament, the New Testament, the Book of Mormon, or the Doctrine and Covenants/Pearl of Great Price.

During the final hour of Sunday church services, men and women separate. Men and boys twelve and older meet in their respective priesthood quorums, while women attend the Relief Society meeting. Lessons are taught and discussions occur which are appropriate to the two genders. Girls age twelve through high school attend young women's classes. Children of both sexes under twelve attend the primary activities.

Two church programs are particularly significant methods for "perfecting the Saints." One is Home Teaching. All families and individual unmarried adults are assigned a home teacher. Ideally, the teacher is actually two priesthood holders, sometimes a father and son, who make at least one monthly visit to the single member or the member family. The purpose of these visits is to act as the bishop's representative and to look after the person's or family's welfare.

Typically, a spiritual lesson is presented, and any concerns the members may have are addressed. The home teacher(s) is also available for emergency assistance should the need arise. Problems that need the attention of the bishop or other priesthood leaders are passed on to them, although in most cases the home teacher(s) handles it himself.

Home teaching is especially important in the case of less active families and individuals. The home teacher may be their only contact with the church, and in most cases he is welcomed for that reason. The primary goal of the home teacher in this situation is to activate or reactivate the family or individual and help them to return to church.

Priesthood home teaching has its counterpart in Relief Society Visiting Teaching. Every adult female church member is assigned a visiting teacher(s) who comes to her home at least once each month and helps to provide spiritual or temporal support.

The other important church program is Family Home Evening. Throughout the church, Monday night of each week is left free for family gatherings and activities. No church meetings or activities are scheduled for this night. Fathers and mothers are urged to gather their children about them, turn off the television or other distractions, and concentrate on and discuss matters of common family concern. A gospel lesson of some kind is usually taught or Scriptures are read, with all members of the family encouraged to both plan and participate. Games may be played and refreshments served. Fun family outings are also appropriate.

Through the Family Home Evening program, family unity is promoted, and children learn to understand and appreciate church standards and gospel principles. When there is a strong Family Home Evening observance in the home, as when children are growing up, they are much less likely to stray in later life.

The family takes first priority in the LDS Church. We have a saying that goes, "No success in life compensates for failure in the home."

Temporal welfare also comes under the church's mission of perfecting the Saints. No one who is truly in need, whether an active or less active church member, is ever denied necessary assistance. In fact, there is probably no parallel religious institution as concerned as the Church of Jesus Christ of Latter-day Saints with sheltering or feeding the needy, caring for the widow and orphan, and even extending assistance to the saving of lives and ameliorating of human suffering throughout the world, regardless of whether the beneficiaries are church-affiliated.

Latter-day Saints in financial difficulty are expected to turn first to their family members or other relatives for assistance, but when this is unavailable they may ask their bishop for help. There is no requirement that they be worthy members in good standing (i.e., tithe payers or living the Word of Wisdom) for this purpose. The only requirement is genuine need.

An eleven-million member church cannot feed and clothe the whole world, of course, but the church makes its limited funds available for relief assistance worldwide following natural disasters or humanitarian crises. These typically take the form of shipments of food and clothing to the affected areas. Somalia and Kosovo were two examples. When disasters occur, such as hurricane Mitch, which struck Central America in 1998, local members and serving missionaries are usually among the first to pitch in and help.

In order to meet a request for financial help, a bishop has available to him the "fast offerings" of his congregation. On the first Sunday of each month, members are asked to fast for two meals and give the money they would otherwise have spent on these meals to the ward fast-offering fund. Those who can afford to do so usually give more than just the cost of the meals missed. The bishop uses these funds for direct monetary assistance to those in need.

There is also the "bishop's storehouse," typically available in larger cities or near concentrations of church members, such as in Utah. Here foodstuffs and sometimes clothing are stored, with the foodstuffs often produced by volunteer member labor on church-owned farms or in canneries. In some cases needy members receive requisitions from their bishops and go directly to the storehouses to pick up their supplies. In most instances home teachers or others will deliver the food or other supplies directly to them in their homes.

The welfare program is not intended to be a substitute for self-reliance. The work ethic is a divinely enshrined church principle, and all who can possibly do so are expected to provide for themselves and their families. Members are encouraged to keep a year's supply of food on hand at all times as a buffer against financial or natural emergencies. The church recognizes, however, that sometimes circumstances beyond one's control dictate the need for temporary help. When those receiving help are healthy and able-bodied, they are sometimes invited to do some kind of work in return—such as repair work on the chapel or work on a farm or cannery. But this is never a requirement for assistance.

Perfecting the Saints also includes healing of the body. Possession of the higher Melchizedek priesthood conveys with it the power to heal. This is one of the great spiritual gifts, as is the faith to be healed on the part of the recipient.

Those who are afflicted physically, or who may be fearful or depressed mentally for any reason, may ask for a healing priesthood blessing, typically from their home teachers. In this case two priesthood holders attend the person. One anoints with consecrated oil, and both then lay their hands on the person's head and pronounce a healing blessing.

These blessings are usually very effective. They are given in combination with, and not as a substitute for, all that medical science can do for the patient. Death comes to all of us, however, and when a person has been "appointed unto death," we recognize that the blessing may be effective only in relieving pain or anxiety.

Healing priesthood blessings are available to all who may request them, members and non-members alike. A father may also give a special priesthood blessing to his children on special occasions, such as blessing and naming them shortly after birth, when they leave home to go to college, or before marriage, or whenever they, or his wife, may desire one.

Church discipline was mentioned earlier, in chapter 4. There are two circumstances under which church courts may be held for disciplinary reasons. One involves serious moral transgressions, such as adultery or gross dishonesty. The other may involve *public* opposition by a member to basic church doctrine, the preaching of false doctrine, or a public disparagement of the church or its leaders.

It is the latter situation that often gets the attention of the media when those so disciplined go public to complain about how they have allegedly been treated.

The Church of Jesus Christ of Latter-day Saints is not a democracy in the usual meaning of that word. There are limits to how far one may go in openly challenging basic church doctrine or policy. But when a person does this, the obvious question would be why he or she would *want* to remain a member.

The great majority of church courts concern immoral actions by members, and the purpose is always to help the person, not to punish him. A court is usually held at the stake level and is conducted by the twelve-member stake High Council, with the stake president presiding. The accused may appear, often accompanied by his bishop, and is offered ample opportunity to defend or explain his actions. A vote is taken concerning the appropriate disciplinary action, if any, which can range from probation to disfellowship and finally, in the most serious of cases, to excommunication. The stake president has the final decision, in consultation with his counselors, and his decision is sustained by the High Council.

Every effort is made, in love, to encourage the person disciplined to repent of his transgression, change his ways, and return to good standing in the church, after an appropriate period of time. The person is never shunned or ostracized in any way. Even those who are excommunicated often change their lives in ways that permit them to recover their church memberships.

The third mission of the church is to redeem the dead. This is a major function of Latter-day Saint temples.

The temple is regarded as the House of the Lord, and is a most sacred place. For Latter-day Saints, the temple is literally the gate to Heaven. Here we are taught eternal principles; here we find a spiritual sanctuary free of all temporal concerns. The goal of every Latter-day Saint is to become worthy to enter the temple. Within the temple walls all members dress in white clothing; there are no differences between rich and poor, prominent and ordinary. All are equal before the Lord.

Temple worship goes back at least as far as the Temple of Solomon, and was the central event in his reign. According to the Talmud, the Temple at Jerusalem, like God's throne and the law (i.e., the Torah) itself, existed before the foundations of the world (*Pesahim* 54a–b).

Temples feature prominently in the Book of Mormon; construction of a temple was a crucial event in the early establishment of the Nephite monarchy after Nephi's separation from his brothers (2 Nephi 5:16–18). Almost from the founding of the church, the Saints were commanded to build temples. The first temple was dedicated in Kirtland, Ohio, on March 27, 1836. One week later, Jesus Christ, the Messiah, appeared in the temple in a vision granted to both Joseph Smith and church leader Oliver Cowdery, and accepted the temple as His house. Moses, Elias, and Elijah then appeared and restored specific priesthood powers.

The word "Elias" has several meanings, including one who is a forerunner or restorer, but in this case Elias appears to have been a man "who committed the dispensation of the gospel of Abraham, saying that in us and our seed all generations after us should be blessed" (Doctrine and Covenants 110:12). Elijah restored the sealing keys, which permit priesthood ordinances performed on earth for the living and the dead to be bound or sealed in Heaven as well, thus helping to turn the hearts of the fathers and children to one another (Malachi 4:5–6). This supreme event is further discussed in chapter 8.

A planned temple in Missouri could not be built because of the persecution there. The beautiful temple in Nauvoo, Illinois, was rushed to completion after the martyrdom of Joseph Smith, even though it was well known that Nauvoo would have to be evacuated because of growing threats of mob violence.

The day after he arrived in the Salt Lake valley on July 24, 1847 (celebrated each year by Latter-day Saint as Pioneer Day), Brigham Young laid out the site for the Salt Lake temple. More than a hundred Latter-day Saint temples are now in operation or are being built throughout the world. The newest ones are much smaller than the temples built in earlier years. The intention is to bring the temple as close as possible to as many members as possible wherever they may live. It is often a great personal and financial sacrifice for members who must travel to temples located far from their homes. This is now changing as more and more temples dot the earth. It took the church 165 years to build the first fifty temples. The next fifty are being dedicated over a period of no more than two or three years.

A Mormon temple is not a Sunday house of worship. Temples are closed on Sundays. Rather, a temple is a place where sacred ordinances are performed, both for the living and for the dead.

Temple ordinances include baptism for the dead, washings and anointings, endowments, and marriages, or "sealings" for eternity.

Couples are married in temples for time and eternity by priesthood holders ("sealers") specially ordained with the power to bind in heaven what is bound on earth. If previously married outside the temple, couples may go there, with their children, and be sealed to each other and to their children for time and eternity. The sealing ordinances are the crowning ordinances of the Gospel and make possible the continuance of the family unit throughout eternity.

The Lord's revelations to the prophet Joseph Smith pertaining to temple ordinances are plainly set forth in the Doctrine and Covenants, section 124:38–42, given in 1841:

> For, for this cause I commanded Moses that he should build a tabernacle, that they should bear it with them in the wilderness, and to build a house in the land of promise, that these ordinances might be revealed which had been hid from before the world was. Therefore, verily I say unto you, that your anointings, and your washings, and your baptisms for the dead, and your solemn assemblies, and your memorials for your sacrifices by the sons of

Levi, and for your oracles in your most holy places wherein you receive conversations, and your statutes, and your judgments, for the beginning of the revelations and foundation of Zion, and for the glory, honor, and endowment of all her municipals, are ordained by the ordinance of my holy house, which my people are always commanded to build unto my holy name. And verily I say unto you, let this house be built unto my name, that I may reveal mine ordinances therein unto my people; For I deign to reveal unto my church things which have been kept hid from before the foundation of the world, things which pertain to the dispensation of the fulness of times. And I will show unto my servant Joseph all things pertaining to this house, and the priesthood thereof, and the place whereon it shall be built.

Thus the sealing ordinances, together with all the other temple ordinances, are also performed for the dead in Latter-day Saint temples. This makes it possible for our Heavenly Father's Plan of Salvation to be effective for all His children who have ever lived, regardless of whether they had the opportunity to hear the Gospel or to be baptized during their mortal lives.

Mormons understand that the Gospel of Jesus Christ is taught in the post-mortal spirit world as well as in mortality. The now disembodied spirits have their moral free agency there as well as on earth to accept or reject it. But baptism, which is essential to exaltation, is an earthly ordinance that can only be performed by the living. Therefore, church members go to holy temples and are baptized in large baptismal fonts as proxies for those who have died. These fonts rest on the backs of twelve oxen symbolically representing the twelve tribes of Israel.

Temple patrons also act as vicarious proxies for the sealing and other necessary earthly ordinances. Washings and anointings are preparatory or initiatory ordinances in the temple. They have biblical precedents (see Exodus 28:41; 1 Kings 1:39, 19:16; 1 Samuel 16:3 for anointings, and Exodus 29:4–7, 30:17–21 for washings). These ordinances, together with the endowment, are performed first for oneself as a living ordinance on the first visit to the temple. Thereafter, on all subsequent visits, the patron serves as a proxy for someone who is dead.

The word "endowment" comes from the first revelation to Joseph Smith concerning temples, which was given at Kirtland, Ohio, on May 6, 1833: "I give unto you a commandment that you should build a house, in which house I design to endow those whom I have chosen with power on high" (Doctrine and Covenants 95:8).

During the endowment ceremony, patrons receive a course of instruction by lectures and visual representations concerning man's eternal journey through mortality. These include a recital of the most prominent events of Creation, a figurative depiction of the advent of Adam and Eve and of every man and every woman, the entry of Adam and Eve into the Garden of Eden, the consequent expulsion from the garden, their condition in the world, and their receiving of the Plan of Salvation leading to the return to the presence of God.[1] In the course of the endowment, patrons also make a series of solemn and sacred covenants with God in the name of Jesus Christ.

Finally, throughout the temple, and especially during the endowment, there is a sense of divine presence. All temple ordinances are seen as a means for receiving inspiration and instruction through the Holy Spirit. As we return to the temple again and again to perform the necessary ordinances for the dead, new spiritual insights often come to us.

Temples themselves are not secret but sacred, as are the ordinances performed in them. Members do not discuss outside the temple the details of what occurs within them, even among themselves. However, temples are open to the public prior to their dedication. Tours are arranged and the general public is invited. After dedication, only Latter-day Saints are admitted who hold temple recommends, which must be renewed annually.

A temple recommend is obtained by means of an interview first with one's bishop and then with the stake president or one of his counselors. Each one signs the recommend. During the interview they ask the member a series of questions regarding his or her allegiance to Jesus Christ, compliance with church standards, and moral worthiness to enter the temple. In this sense it might be said

---

[1] James E. Talmadge, *House of the Lord*, pp. 83–84.

that only members in good standing are eligible to go to the temple.

Temple work for the dead, that is, redeeming the dead, can only be carried out if the dead can be identified. Therefore Latter-day Saints usually spend much time doing genealogical research in order to trace their ancestral lines, and then perform, or allow others to perform, the temple ordinances for their ancestors. Otherwise, when they go to the temple they take a name supplied to them by the temple from someone else's genealogical work and perform the ordinances for that person. Such names are also often obtained by going through census and other records as part of a name-extraction program carried out by church members throughout the world.

In the course of this extraction program, the names of some Jewish Holocaust victims were obtained in the past and temple ordinances were performed on their behalf. This caused a considerable objection by some Jews who were offended by the notion that the church was trying to make Mormons out of their deceased relatives. As mentioned above, this would not be possible without the post-mortal consent of those affected, but the church acknowledged Jewish sensibilities and agreed to cease baptizing known Jewish dead without the consent of their living relatives or descendants.

The ideal standard for Latter-day Saints is to be *in* the world but not *of* the world. This means that Latter-day Saints mingle and associate freely with those not of their faith but, ideally, try to avoid worldly lifestyles that tend to stifle spiritual growth and impede their eternal progress.

Two General Conferences are held each year in the Salt Lake Conference Center and broadcast by satellite to church members all over the world. During these two-day conferences, all the members of the First Presidency and the Quorum of the Twelve speak, as well as some of the other general authorities and women auxiliary leaders. The talks provide inspired counsel on many subjects, including, especially, how to live better, more Christ-like lives. The standards set are high, but they are not impossible to achieve.

Mormonism's concept of moral and ethical standards tends to be less situational than absolute. As between moral relativism and moral absolutism, we come down hard on the latter side. For us the commandments of God are more than suggestions. Because Mormons are human like everyone else, not all members will always live up to the high standards set by the church (and by God). It is perhaps an honor (of sorts!) that when one of us does transgress in some public fashion, the fact that he or she is a Mormon will often be mentioned in the media account of the matter. At least we consider it an honor that the world knows of our high ethical standards and perhaps expects more of us for that reason than it does of others.

We Mormons are not automatons, however, who blindly follow our leaders in all things. Obedience to the law of the Gospel and to the commandments of our Heavenly Father is fundamental to our eternal progression, but so is the exercise of our free agency. We do not find these principles contradictory.

Mormons are urged to follow the inspired counsel of those called by God to be their leaders. However, God specifically warned, by revelation, against the exercise of unrighteous dominion:

> Behold, there are many called, but few are chosen, and why are they not chosen? Because their hearts are set so much upon the things of this world, and aspire to the honors of men, that they do not learn this one lesson—That the rights of the priesthood are inseparably connected with the powers of heaven, and that the powers of heaven cannot be controlled nor handled only upon the principle of righteousness. That they may be conferred upon us, it is true; but when we undertake to cover our sins, or to gratify our pride, our vain ambition, or to exercise control or dominion or compulsion upon the souls of the children of men, in any degree of unrighteousness, behold, the heavens withdraw themselves; the Spirit of the Lord is grieved; and when it is withdrawn, Amen to the priesthood or the authority of that man.
> (Doctrine and Covenants 121:34–37)

From these words it is apparent that obedience is to righteousness, and not to individuals, and that it is our privilege to exercise our own discernment as to the correctness—in terms of the divine will—of whatever we may be asked to do or believe. A church leader, for example, who asked or suggested that we vote in a certain way or for a particular person or party would be acting very inappropriately and undoubtedly would be censured for so doing. Likewise, since there has been no revelation given concerning the *method* by which God organized the bodies of Adam and Eve, any statement made by a church leader on the subject of organic evolution (and there have been many!) would be only his opinion, and would not be binding in any way on the individual beliefs (which may vary greatly) of the members of the church.

The principle of obedience to God and His commandments, however, is often cited by Latter-day Saints from the Hebrew Bible. The quotation is from the admonition of the prophet Samuel to King Saul, after the latter failed to fully obey the words of the Lord conveyed to him by Samuel: "Hath the Lord as great delight in burnt offering and sacrifices, as in obeying the voice of the Lord? Behold, to obey is better than sacrifice, and to hearken than the fat of rams" (1 Samuel 15:22 KJV).

Chapter 7

Differences and Similarities

This book deals with Judaism and Mormonism on their own terms. Our thesis is that Jews need to know more about Mormonism, and Mormons about Judaism. We have included some of the traditional Mormon polemics regarding Judaism in order to convey to the Jewish reader the Mormon tradition regarding Judaism and why there is a felt need to convert Jews, an attitude not reciprocated by Judaism vis-à-vis Mormonism. The purpose of this book is to foster increased understanding between the adherents of these two religions.

One of the best ways to do this, beyond describing how each religion functions and some of its fundamental beliefs, is to look at the major differences between the two religions as well as at some of the similarities. We do this not to suggest that the similarities make them the same, but to note some of the salient differences even within the similarities.

Both Judaism and Christianity, and Mormonism as a form of the latter, use the Hebrew Bible as one of the bases for their religious attitudes and beliefs. For all intents and purposes, the Hebrew Bible and the Christian Old

Testament are the same body of sacred literature, although there is a different sequence of books, and of course, many differences of interpretation, translation, and emphasis.

In addition to the Hebrew Bible, or Old Testament, the sacred literature of Christianity includes the New Testament, plus an extensive collection of writings by Christian clerics and thinkers over the centuries, many of which Mormonism does not accept. On the other hand, in addition to the New Testament, Mormonism has the Book of Mormon, the Doctrine and Covenants, and the Pearl of Great Price. These writings are integral to the Mormon tradition, but are not found in Judaism or in other branches of Christianity.

When a Christian cites his own sacred literature in discussion with Jews in order to prove a theological point, there is often a failure of communication. Jews do not accept Christian Scripture. Unfortunately Christians seldom recognize this problem, as Mr. Johnson has at times found in presenting his Mormonism to Rabbi Leffler. The accepted literatures are just not the same, even though they begin with the same basic text. The comparison here might be to a Muslim quoting from the Koran to prove a point to a Christian.

The next body of religious literature in Judaism after the Bible is the Mishnah, a codification of laws and traditions based upon the biblical interpretations of the Pharisees and the earliest rabbis. The Mishnah is, in essence, the first literature of the Oral Torah, and the first Jewish example of the proof-text methodology. The same method is used in the New Testament, which apparently emerged from the Pharisaic tradition of biblical interpretation, as shown by its frequent use of Bible quotations to prove its assertions about Jesus. The Mishnah was compiled around the year 200 C.E. and contains the discussions and opinions of the earliest rabbis, a title which only came into use in Judaism after the destruction of the Temple in Jerusalem in the year 70 C.E.

Three hundred years later the Gemara was compiled. Whereas the Mishnah is in Hebrew, the Gemara is in Aramaic, the spoken language of the Near East at the time. It is an extensive commentary on the Mishnah with discussions ranging across the full spectrum of contemporary life. This massive tome of many volumes, together with the Mishnah, is known as the Talmud. In the centuries following its compilation, many commentaries were written about it to further explain unclear passages.

In addition, there also developed a body of literature known as Midrash, of which there are many volumes. The Midrash incorporates rabbinic commentary on Scripture, often verse by verse, and is primarily of a sermonic nature (an extract from the Midrash on Psalm 9 will be found in Appendix 2). It pulls together various texts to gain new insights and understanding from Scripture, using the proof-text method, which combines a number of texts—frequently not in context—to develop a new idea or belief. The Midrash may present three or more interpretations of the same verse, any of which may be used when appropriate, or not used if inappropriate.

Jewish tradition further includes a wealth of other literature that attempts to explain and illuminate the meaning of the biblical text, both passages that deal with ritual behavior (such as the red heifer in the Midrash on Psalm 9 in the appendix) as well as those that deal with ideas relating to God and human situations. All of this literature is considered Oral Torah, teaching after the time of the Bible. It is ongoing revelation in the Jewish sense and very different from the Mormon understanding of modern revelation through prophets, seers, and revelators, so much so, indeed, that they cannot really be compared.

As the foregoing summary should make obvious, Judaism is not dependent upon the literature of any other religion. It is complete within itself and does not utilize sacred texts from another tradition as part of its holy writ. Thus it stands alone, not needing to rely on any Scripture associated with another religion, as Christianity does with the Hebrew Bible.

This is a major difference between Judaism and Christianity, and unfortunately again, one often overlooked by both Jews and Christians in dialogue. It accounts for Judaism's not having to interpret the Scripture of another religious tradition to build its own message as Christianity does. This difference brings about much misunderstanding, as we mentioned above. The problem becomes especially evident when adherents of another religion use its literature in discussions with Jews, expecting them to know and accept it—an approach that both traditional Christianity and Mormonism have historically taken. From a Jewish standpoint, this makes no sense and is even resented.

The problem becomes most obvious when Jews encounter the Christian missionary agenda. Judaism has not been conversionist for many centuries. We believe our religion is complete unto itself and fully adequate for our needs. And since Judaism's message does not depend on the interpretation of another religion's literature to prove its position, we feel no need to convince others of Judaism's religious truths (i.e., what is true for us) and insights by seeking to convert them to Judaism in order to support our interpretation.

In sharp contrast, in historical Christianity, and even today in some Christian denominations, such as the Southern Baptists, the conversion of Jews has been an important agenda item. This is true of Mormonism also, as will be evident in the next chapter of this book. Here then is a major difference between the two religions and one that needs to be understood by Jews, even when we disagree and take offense when Mormons seek to convert us. And it should be understood as well by those Mormons who seek to convert us.

Perhaps one of the most salient similarities but differences that comes out of these different literary traditions is the belief in the Messiah. Christianity proclaims that Jesus was the Messiah, or Christ. Judaism declares that God has yet to bring either the Messiah or the messianic age (see the reference to this in the Midrash on Psalm 9). The world is yet to be redeemed, as we noted in our consideration of the idea of redemption in the Siddur. Human struggle and conflict have not ceased. Nonetheless, each religion has its own rationale for proclaiming its beliefs regarding the Messiah which come out of its own traditions. Thus in its own context each religion's assertions make sense. Our intent here is not to argue the point but to enlighten the reader, although the next chapter may not seem so even-handed to some Jews.

A belief in a future leader who will come and bring deliverance to the world, a Messiah, is not inherent in any one biblical text. It requires the weaving together of many different passages (the proof-texting methodology mentioned above) in order to develop such a belief. Judaism and Christianity use many of the same biblical texts to do this but interpret them very differently.

The idea of the Messiah is not as precisely defined in Judaism as it is in Christianity. This is primarily because Christianity—as its very name makes clear—focuses on Jesus as the Messiah, or Christ, while Judaism has never made the belief in a Messiah the core of its religious message and beliefs. Nonetheless there have been times when the Jewish messianic hope was very prominent, perhaps most notably in the seventeenth century, when Shabbetai Zvi, in Turkey, proclaimed himself the long-awaited Messiah and attracted many followers. Many of these people were subsequently disillusioned and converted to Islam, as he did.

Since Judaism, as we indicated at the beginning of this book, begins with a theophany of a religious people at

Mount Sinai and not with a theological statement, the acceptance or non-acceptance of a messianic belief is not a test of being Jewish. Consequently there has been a great deal of latitude in regard to how the Messiah is envisioned.

Nonetheless, certain general messianic beliefs are commonly held within the Jewish tradition. The Messiah is to usher in a period of universal peace and well-being when there will no longer be war and human suffering, when men will "beat their swords into plowshares, and their spears into pruning hooks" (Isaiah 2:4, Micah 4:13).

The Messiah will be a charismatic human leader, the scion of the House of David, and with God's assistance, he will bring about this marvelous time for all humanity, starting with the Jewish people and bringing them all (both the living and the dead) back to Jerusalem. How this feat is to be accomplished is God's doing. It was never spelled out in any detail.

Some rabbis held there would be two Messiahs: the coming of the greater of them, the Messiah Son of David, would be preceded by the advent of the Messiah Son of Joseph, who would bring about a great war, and only after that war would the true Messiah, the Son of David, be able to prevail. Other rabbis did not believe in the need for the Messiah, the Son of Joseph, but believed that the Messiah would come in God's own time and as He so directed, a reflection of the both/and approach.

Regardless of the specifics of belief about the Messiah per se, and his appearance, he would not be a god incarnate, as Christianity has depicted Jesus, but only a great human being, the product of God's hand in human affairs.

The lack of God's bringing about a Messiah or messianic age as anticipated is the reason that one ultra-Orthodox Hasidic group in Israel today so strongly opposes the very existence of that secular nation. They refuse to have any part in it, even refusing to speak Hebrew, the language of the state, because they regard it as a holy tongue not to be used for secular purposes. They view the state as a blasphemy because it is the product of human effort and not of divine origin, but they are in a distinct minority.

On the other hand, there are traditionalist Jews who view the establishment of the State of Israel and its subsequent history as a precursor of the coming of the Messiah, a view which is found in some Christian groups and associated with the second coming of Jesus. As is so typical in Judaism, there is no consensus here, and we are able to encompass those varying opinions because of our both/and outlook.

Today modernist Jews no longer look for the Messiah as a person, but rather for a messianic age, a time when God will bring about the end of human suffering, war, and distress. At the same time, some Lubavitcher Hasidim, a sect of Orthodox Judaism, believe that their late leader, Rabbi Menachem Schneerson, who died a few years ago and was their chief rabbi, was the Messiah.

Because of Judaism's openness to differing religious opinions within the parameters of Jewish belief, these kinds of differences can and do occur. They are not a reason for exclusion from Judaism but give it variety.

Nonetheless, there are parameters for exclusion. And when a person steps outside these parameters as generally held by the Jewish people, as with the wicked son in the Passover Seder whom we mentioned earlier, he excludes himself from his people; he has become an apostate, even if he declares that he does not believe that he has done so. This is the situation with any group or person that declares that one can be Jewish and at the same time hold a belief in Jesus as the Messiah, a doctrine central to Christianity and totally rejected by Judaism. To many Christians this parameter is confusing because, as we have pointed out, Judaism does not require theological conformity or agreement to be a Jew. Nonetheless the affirmation of the core belief of another religion is beyond the parameter.

When a Jew accepts Jesus he becomes a Christian, as do his descendants. Judaism becomes a family memory, no longer a living, vital religion for them. Such persons have converted, in spite of any protestation either by them or the religion to which they have converted. Thus while the Jews for Jesus or even Jews who become Mormons may still think of themselves as Jews, their actions and involvement in their new religious life will pull them away from the Jewish community over time and bring them and their family fully into Christianity.

As we indicated at the beginning of this book, more often than not (with the exception of converts) Jews are born into their religion. At least one of his parents (histor-ically, the mother; but in modern times, in some traditions, also the father) was Jewish, and he was raised as a Jew.

In another chapter we mention the *B'rit Milah* cere-mony, the ritual circumcision, and the hopes expressed in it for the eight-day-old infant. These are but two exam-ples of the sense of religious continuity which is very much a part of Jewish tradition and which is not found in Mormonism, where individual choice of religion is emphasized.

This sense of continuity extends from the biblical past until today and is central to the hope for the future, for the maintenance of the people and its covenant with God into all succeeding generations. Concern for the future continuity of Judaism is a frequent agenda item at Jewish meetings. The apostate has broken the continuity.

The former Christian who becomes a Jew does not have the same ambiguity of being a part of two religions. He no longer considers himself a Christian—part Christian/part Jew. He has converted to Judaism, and his former religion is no longer a part of his religious life. He has severed all active ties to it.

In part this difference occurs because the Christian is not born a Christian. He has to be brought into the church either by infant or youth baptism, as practiced in some churches, or by declaring his belief in Jesus as the Messiah and then being baptized into the church of his choice as an adult. This ceremony initiates him into his religion. As a result, there is not the same sense of religious continuity (except where nationalism and religion have become intermingled) that one finds in Judaism. This is a significant difference and one that is often not appreciated or recognized by Christians, especially in the United States, where the mingling of nationality and religion has not occurred.

Another area of difference and similarity is the antagonism that each religion has experienced. Until modern times and the rise of nationalism, anti-Jewish sentiments in Christendom were often based on either theological grounds or economic opportunism. The former occurred when Christians felt insecure and challenged by the Jewish denial of their messianic claims regarding Jesus. The latter occurred when Christian rulers were jealous of Jewish wealth and used the church as a cohort in extorting money from their Jewish subjects. The Inquisition in Spain in the fourteenth and fifteenth centuries held elements of both reasons.

With the rise of modern nationalism, anti-Jewish activity moved from its earlier rationale to an involvement with supposed national or even "racial" purity. It became what we now call anti-Semitism. Jews were viewed as aliens within the society in which they lived, even after many generations of living there. They were not considered true Germans or Russians, for instance, but foreigners. This process began with Napoleon, continued in tsarist Russia, and reached its zenith with Hitler and the Holocaust.

There has also been a history of anti-Semitism in the United States (a nation of immigrants), perhaps not as virulent as in other countries, but we Jews have experienced it here, with exclusion from resorts, with quotas for acceptance at many colleges and universities, with severe restrictions on Jews in certain professions and neighborhoods. While most of these situations are no longer operative, there are still instances of overt desecration of synagogues and Jewish cemeteries. Anti-Semitism is still found in anti-Jewish expressions, anti-Jewish symbols scrawled on walls, and ongoing hate crimes.

In contrast, anti-Mormonism, which originally was manifested in violent and often deadly demonstrations against Mormons, in more recent times tends to be the product of people who actively try to disprove Mormon beliefs. This activity is usually done with the publication of tracts that attempt to disprove Mormon interpretations of Scripture and demonstrate that the Book of Mormon is false. These efforts tend to be theological attacks and disputations. They are no longer of a physical nature as they were in the nineteenth century. Anti-Mormonism has a far more limited scope today than in the past. Thus, while both religions have known antagonism, they have each experienced it, and continue to experience it, in manifestly different ways.

Another, and profound, difference between Judaism and Mormonism is in how each religion looks at ethical questions. As Mr. Johnson mentioned, Judaism, contrary to Mormonism, does not have an absolutist approach to ethics. In Judaism, ethics are part of the halachic system. There are forbidden actions, such as murder, adultery, and idol worship, and there are obligations (mitzvot), such as assisting the poor, clothing the naked, and honoring one's parents. However, in between the forbidden acts and the religious obligations there are many actions and ethical decisions in life which are in neither category. Some of these are of far-reaching proportions; to name but a few, the area of medical ethics (which is becoming more and more complex due to advances in medical technology and certain social questions that arise as a result), the ethics of business and commerce, and various questions raised by international terrorism.

Halachah addresses these many issues by looking at Jewish tradition to find out how similar questions were considered in the past and then inferring answers to the modern question that are consonant with tradition but appropriate to contemporary needs. With centuries of rabbinic discussion on so many different ethical subjects, there is a wealth of literature to which to turn for insight and direction. And from these writings there has developed an extensive literature known as responsa. This consists of questions posed by Jews in various communities to the leading halachic scholars of their time and the responses which these rabbis gave as a result of their searching through Jewish sources, both the Written and the Oral Torah, dealing with whatever was the subject of the question (two examples of modern rabbinic responses to ethical questions of this kind are included in Appendix 3).

Since Halachah deals with every facet of life, so too does the responsa literature. Thus, what to the Mormon may appear to be a relativistic approach to ethics has, nevertheless, the guidelines of a rich tradition from which to seek answers to life's questions dealing with what is to be considered appropriate behavior in any given situation. Thus in Judaism most ethical questions do not have a straightforward right or wrong response, as is so typical in Mormonism. They require an in-depth inquiry as to what is appropriate and what is inappropriate behavior, and the Halachah provides this resource.

There is yet another difference that ought not to be overlooked in this chapter—leadership. Judaism has not had an officiating priesthood since the destruction of the Temple in Jerusalem by the Romans in the year 70 C.E. Since then the leadership has been in the hands of rabbis, a title that came into use after the fall of Jerusalem and literally means "my teacher."

A rabbi is a person with many years of intensive study and training in Jewish texts and tradition. Historically he was a teacher of Judaism, as the title indicates, and not a preacher. However, in modern America he has come to function in a ministerial capacity in the synagogue. Among his duties, in addition to conducting worship services, is the responsibility to teach Judaism to the congregation, and in this role he is often called upon to bring the nuances of the Jewish tradition to bear upon current situations. To do this he uses the wealth of Jewish learning he has acquired to provide insight, guidance, and understanding of modern questions as seen through the historical texts of his religion, thereby, in his own way, adding to the tradition of Oral Torah. While the rabbinate in former times was strictly a male function, there are now women rabbis in the Reform and the Conservative movements.

In many respects, then, Judaism is still developing, bringing its insights and awareness from the past to shed light upon life today. This process is, in essence, part of the tradition of Oral Torah as we have considered it in this book. This "revelation" is ongoing, continually renewed in each generation as rabbis and scholars search the texts for an ever increasing understanding of God and His desires for us as His children.

In some respects, this is akin to the Mormon belief in an ongoing revelation which seeks an ever increasing understanding of the religious message. But they are also vastly different. Mormons believe that God is still speaking to them through their prophets and thus revealing new truths. Judaism does not codify the teachings of its latter-day teachers, but merely places them in the tradition of Jewish learning and interpretation as modern-day Oral Torah. Nevertheless, both religions remain open to growth and insight.

Chapter 8

Mormonism and the House of Israel

Revelation from God comes in different ways, both to prophets and to individuals. It is spiritual in nature rather than physical, and the recipient must be spiritually attuned and receptive. Sometimes it may come in the form of an impression or prompting upon the mind, often while studying or pondering the Scriptures. At other times it may occur as a "still small voice," or even an audible voice. It may come to us through dreams, or even waking visions. It may not always come in ways that are unmistakable to us or as we might expect or desire. A former president and prophet of the church, Spencer W. Kimball, once said about revelation to prophets, "The great volume of revelation ... comes to today's prophets in the less spectacular way—that of deep impressions but without spectacle or glamour or dramatic events accompanying."[1]

Sometimes, however, revelation may come to prophets by means of supernal visions during which there is direct and unmistakable communication from deity. Such was the case when Moses encountered Jehovah on Mount

---

[1] *Instructor*, August 1960, p. 257.

Sinai, and again when the boy prophet Joseph Smith was visited by both the Father and the Son at Palmyra, New York, in 1820. These are theophanies, the rarest of all divine interventions in human affairs. The Church of Jesus Christ of Latter-day Saints records in its early history a number of such direct heavenly visitations.

Latter-day Saints consider themselves to be members of the House of Israel and apply the name "Israel" to themselves. They do this, in part, because of a particularly great and magnificent revelatory vision granted to Joseph Smith and his associate Oliver Cowdery on April 3, 1836 (Passover time).

The place was the Kirtland, Ohio, temple. Before the eyes of these two men the Lord Jehovah (Jesus Christ), Moses, Elias, *and the prophet Elijah* all appeared, one after the other. In Joseph Smith's account of this event:

> After this vision [of Jehovah] closed, the heavens were again opened unto us: and Moses appeared before us, and committed unto us the keys of the gathering of Israel from the four parts of the earth, and the leading of the ten tribes from the land of the north. After this, Elias appeared, and committed the dispensation of the gospel of Abraham, saying that in us and in our seed all generations after us should be blessed. After this vision had closed another great and glorious vision burst upon us; for Elijah the prophet, who was taken to heaven without tasting death, stood before us and

said: Behold the time has fully come, which was spoken of by the mouth of Malachi—testifying that he [Elijah] should be sent, before the great and dreadful day of the Lord come—To turn the hearts of the fathers to the children and the children to the fathers, lest the whole earth be smitten with a curse.

(Doctrine and Covenants 110:11–15)

Jews still await the return of Elijah. Rabbi Leffler has described this anticipation as part of the Passover Seder. But to us Mormons, he has *already* returned. *We consider that this great event links us inseparably with the House of Israel.*

Latter-day Saints also learn from the revelation given in their patriarchal blessings that they are descendants of the tribes of Israel, either literally by blood or by adoption at baptism. This is yet another major reason why we consider ourselves to be a part of the House of Israel.

We Mormons consider Genesis and Exodus to be not only religious history but literal history. In this sense we are quite similar to traditionalist Jews, though not necessarily to the modernist Jews represented by Rabbi Leffler. Genesis is mostly a series of biographical accounts, probably written by the patriarchs from Adam down through Ephraim. Moses probably had access to these records, which were possibly sealed up with the bones of Joseph and carried with the Children of Israel to the Promised Land. Therefore, he may have abridged them, much as

Mormon did with the records kept by Book of Mormon prophets.

Modern revelation confirms and amplifies the biblical accounts of Moses' intimate association with deity, and his role as seer, liberator, lawgiver, and leader of Israel, as well as his connection with the books of the Pentateuch, or Written Torah, as Judaism calls the first five books of the Bible.

The Book of Moses, included in the Pearl of Great Price, constitutes a portion of Joseph Smith's inspired translation of the Bible, mentioned earlier in this book. As such, it is a much more complete account of the earth's creation process than has come down to us in the biblical version found in Genesis. It is an account of the visions given to Moses on a high mountain before he led Israel out of Egypt (Moses, chap. 1). These visions and revelations were received separately from the Ten Commandments. The visions have five themes: (1) the greatness of God in comparison to humans; (2) Jesus Christ as the only Begotten Son and creator of "worlds without number"; (3) Satan and his opposition to the divine plan; (4) the spiritual nature of Moses; and (5) the purposes of God, stated in Moses 1:39: "This is my work and my glory, to bring about the eternal life and immortality of man."

Genesis provides the blood-line genealogy of the patriarchs, but does not give their priesthood genealogy. The Doctrine and Covenants reveals that Moses received the holy priesthood from his father-in-law Jethro, who

was a descendant of Abraham. Abraham in turn received
the priesthood from Melchizedek, who received it from
his fathers back to Noah, and from Noah to Enoch and
back to Adam (Doctrine and Covenants 84:6–17).

The Joseph Smith Translation tells us much more
about Melchizedek than does the Hebrew Bible (Genesis
14:18–20). It includes an additional sixteen verses that
provide these details. We learn that Melchizedek was
ordained a high priest after "the order of the son of God."
He was a prophet similar to Enoch, who had power,
through his faith, over the elements, and over the nations
of the earth, and the power to stand in the presence of
God. He was called by his people the Prince of Peace.
Abraham sought out Melchizedek and was himself
ordained a high priest after the order of the Son of God.
The Joseph Smith Translation further records, "His
[Melchizedek's] people wrought righteousness, and
obtained heaven, and sought for the city of Enoch which
God had before taken, separating it from the earth, having
reserved it unto the latter days, or the end of the world"
(Genesis 14:34).

These verses remind us of the power of a priesthood
hierarchy: that Abraham received the priesthood from an
authorized servant of the Lord, that he paid his tithing to
him, and that Melchizedek had the power to bless
Abraham in accordance with the covenants the Lord had
made with Abraham.[2] Modern revelation thus fills in the

---

[2]See *Ensign of the Church of Jesus Christ of Latter-Day Saints*, August
1997, p. 14.

many gaps and uncertainties that exist in the Hebrew Bible.

The priesthood is mentioned in the preceding chapters and above, but the Latter-day Saint understanding of the priesthood needs now to be more fully discussed.

Joseph Smith defined priesthood as "an everlasting principle [which has] existed with God from eternity, and will to eternity . . . holding the key of power and blessings. In fact, Priesthood is a perfect law of theocracy."[3]

Brigham Young defined it this way:

> If anybody wants to know what the Priesthood of the Son of God is, it is the law by which the worlds are, were, and will continue forever and ever. It is that system which brings worlds into existence and peoples them, gives them their revolutions—their days, weeks, months, years, their seasons and times, and by which they are rolled up into a scroll, as it were, and go into a higher state of existence. . . . This Priesthood has been on the earth at various times. Adam had it, Seth had it, Enoch had it, Noah had it, Abraham and Lot had it, and it was handed down to the days of the Prophets, long after the days of the ancients. This High Priesthood rules, directs, governs, and controls all the Priesthoods, because it is the highest of all.[4]

---

[3] *Teachings of the Prophet Joseph Smith*, pp. 157, 322.
[4] *Discourses of Brigham Young*, pp. 130–131.

Latter-day Saints understand priesthood to have four meanings: (1) Priesthood is *power*, the power of God delegated to men to act in all things for the benefit of mankind, both in the world and out of it. (2) Priesthood is *authority*, the exclusive right to act in the name of God as His authorized agents, and to perform ordinances for the purpose of opening certain spiritual blessings to all individuals. (3) Priesthood is the right and responsibility to *preside* within the organizational structure of the church. (4) Sometimes the word "priesthood" is used to refer to the men of the church in general.

Thus the priesthood is all-embracing and involves all forms of God's power. It is the means by which all the worlds throughout the universe were created and ordered. It is the channel for receiving revelation, and thus the method through which God reveals Himself and His purposes to mankind. When employed by His servants in His service, it is as if by the Lord's own mouth:

> What I the Lord have spoken, I have spoken, and I excuse not myself; and though the heavens and the earth pass away, my word shall not pass away, but shall all be fulfilled, whether by mine own voice or the voice of my servants it is the same.
>
> (Doctrine and Covenants 1:38)

The priesthood, as it is understood anciently, and functions today in the Church of Jesus Christ of Latter-day Saints, is neither professional nor hereditary, nor is it held by a group of specialists. Unlike the case in ancient times, it no longer involves sacrificial rites, neither actually, as described in the Hebrew Bible, nor symbolically, as in Roman Catholicism. One does not assume it in any automatic way, unless it is revealed in his patriarchal blessing that a man is directly descended from the tribe of Levi. Apart from this extremely rare exception, one must be ordained to the priesthood by one having the authority to do so. All worthy Mormon men are eligible to hold the priesthood.

There are two priesthoods within the Church of Jesus Christ of Latter-day Saints.

The lesser, or Aaronic priesthood, which carries the authority to baptize, is generally held by all worthy young men aged twelve through eighteen or nineteen, and by some adults. A young man is first ordained to the office of deacon when he turns twelve. Other offices within the Aaronic priesthood are teacher (age fourteen to sixteen), and priest (sixteen and older).

Latter-day Saints' insights into the origins of the Aaronic priesthood stem from modern revelations, indicating that when Moses led Israel out of Egypt, the Lord intended to confer upon worthy men of all tribes the higher Melchizedek priesthood. Disobedience, however, caused the Israelites to harden their hearts against the Lord and Moses. Therefore, the Lord eventually

took Moses out of their midst, and the Holy Priesthood also; and the lesser priesthood holdeth

the key of the ministering of angels and the preparatory Gospel; which Gospel is the Gospel of repentance and of baptism, and the remission of sins, and the law of carnal commandments, which the Lord in his wrath caused to continue with the house of Aaron among the children of Israel until John [the Baptist], whom God raised up.
(Doctrine and Covenants 84:25–27)

The Aaronic priesthood is sometimes referred to as the Levitical priesthood. To assist Aaron and his sons, other worthy male members of the tribe of Levi were also given authority in the lesser priesthood. In the strict sense, the Levitical priesthood is a lesser part of the Aaronic priesthood, held among those who were Levites but not of the family of Aaron. The Doctrine and Covenants states that "there are, in the Church, two priesthoods, namely, the Melchizedek and Aaronic, including the Levitical Priesthood" (Doctrine and Covenants 107:1). The Aaronic priesthood was restored to the earth in May of 1829, by an angel, later identified as John the Baptist. He appeared to Joseph Smith and Oliver Cowdery on the banks of the Susquehanna River, and conveyed to them the authority to baptize each other.

The higher, or Melchizedek, priesthood incorporates all priesthoods within itself. It contains the offices of elder and high priest. From Adam down to Moses, all of the prophet/patriarchs, including Seth, Enoch, Noah, Abraham, Isaac, Jacob, and Joseph, held the Melchizedek priesthood. The name Melchizedek is shorthand for "the

Holy Priesthood after the Order of the Son of God." To avoid too frequent use of the name of deity, this priesthood is given the name of the great "priest of the most high God," Melchizedek.

Abraham presumably received his priesthood from Melchizedek because his own father was unworthy. Joseph Smith taught that the prophets after the time of Christ held this same priesthood and were "ordained by God Himself."[5] Under the patriarchal order from Adam to Abraham, the birthright normally went to the oldest son, and with it the conveyance, by the father's blessing, of the Melchizedek priesthood. From Abraham to Ephraim (Joseph's younger son), the birthright blessing went to the younger sons because of their righteousness.

The Melchizedek priesthood was lost to the earth following the death of the apostles. It was restored to the earth in June 1829, by the appearance of the apostles Peter, James, and John, who conferred it upon Joseph Smith and Oliver Cowdery.

The Bible tells us little concerning the earlier patriarchs prior to Abraham, except that their righteousness set a pattern referred to in later generations. The books of Abraham and Moses in the Pearl of Great Price reveal more of the visions, revelations, ordinations, and divine experiences of many of these ancient priesthood holders.

Unofficially, Latter-day Saint commentators refer to seven major "dispensations" of time, named after the prin-

---

[5] *Teachings of the Prophet Joseph Smith*, p. 181.

cipal prophet of each: Adam, Enoch, Noah, Abraham, Moses, Jesus Christ (who led the dispensation of the Meridian of Time), and Joseph Smith (who introduced the dispensation of the Fullness of Time). A dispensation of the Gospel is a period in which the Lord has at least one authorized servant on the earth who bears the holy priesthood and the keys, and who has a divine commission to dispense the Gospel to the inhabitants of the earth. The existence of priesthood authority is thus common to all dispensations.

The Church of Jesus Christ of Latter-day Saints claims to be a restoration of the covenants made by God with Abraham, Isaac, and Jacob. From our very beginning we have had a deep interest in the remnant of the House of Israel, the descendants of Judah. Latter-day Saints consider Israel to be, indeed, a Chosen People. We cite Exodus 19:5–6:

> Now, therefore, if ye will obey my voice indeed, and keep my covenant, then ye shall be a peculiar treasure unto me above all people: for all the earth is mine: And ye shall be unto me a kingdom of priests, and an holy nation.

At the time of the divided monarchy, Israelite prophets pleaded with the people to keep their neglected covenants with God in order to assure His continued protection. Isaiah warned that the Assyrian army would become "the rod of [God's] anger" (Isaiah 10:5). After they rejected those prophetic warnings, both Israel and Judah were conquered and scattered. This first scattering of Israel occurred first when the Assyrians carried away the ten northern tribes into captivity (ca. 722 B.C.). The second phase was the Babylonian captivity of the kingdom of Judah (ca. 587 B.C.), shortly after Lehi and his family fled from Jerusalem. The third phase was the destruction of the Jewish state and the Second Temple by the Romans (66–70 A.D.).

As a consequence of this scattering, the blood of Israel has presumably been mixed in with most of the peoples of the earth. The Book of Mormon speaks of this scattering. Lehi's son, the prophet Nephi, writing in the Americas, noted that his people were part of a scattered Israel that would one day be gathered:

> . . . for it appears that the house of Israel, sooner or later, will be scattered upon all the face of the earth, and also among all nations. . . . And after our seed is scattered the Lord God will . . . bring them again out of captivity, and they shall be gathered together to the lands of their inheritance; and they shall be brought out of obscurity and out of darkness; and they shall know that the Lord is their Savior and their Redeemer, the Mighty One of Israel.
>
> (1 Nephi 22:3, 7, 12)

Latter-day Saints are interested in the scattering of Israel primarily because of the gathering of Israel that is prophesied to occur in the latter days. We consider that this gathering began in 1829 when the priesthood was restored to the earth through the prophet Joseph Smith. The appearance of Moses in the Kirtland temple, who at that time gave the keys, or authorization, for the gathering of Israel to Joseph Smith and Oliver Cowdery, was a signal event of the Restoration. Today Latter-day Saint missionaries, commissioned by those with priesthood authority, gather latter-day Israel back to the covenant and acceptance of their Redeemer.

The term "latter-day Israel" does not necessarily mean only modern-day Jews, although of course Jews are taught whenever they care to listen (and *only* then). It means, rather, Israel in the broadest sense, which we define to include all the worthy descendants of Abraham. They are taught now in all of the nations to which their ancestors were long ago dispersed.

The ten lost tribes of Israel, that is, those carried into captivity by the Assyrians, feature prominently in Latter-day Saint thinking and doctrine as Israelites other than either the Jews or the Lamanites of the Book of Mormon. The Lamanites were the survivors of the climactic battle with the Nephites recounted in the Book of Mormon, and thus today include many of the native peoples of the Western Hemisphere. They are the descendants of Joseph through both Manasseh and Ephraim, since Lehi was a descendant of Manasseh, and Ishmael, another member of the original landing party, was of the tribe of Ephraim. The Book of the Mormon prophet Nephi, the righteous younger son of Lehi, speaking as the mouthpiece of the

Lord, stated that the Lord had not forgotten the ten tribes:

> For behold I shall speak unto the Jews and they
> shall write it; and I shall speak unto the Nephites
> and they shall write it; and I shall speak unto the
> other tribes of the House of Israel, which I have
> led away, and they shall write it; and I shall speak
> unto all nations of the earth and they shall write it.
> . . . and the Jews shall have the words of the lost
> tribes of Israel; and the lost tribes shall have the
> words of the Nephites and the Jews. And it shall
> come to pass that my people, which are of the
> house of Israel, shall be gathered home to the land
> of their possessions; and my word shall be gathered
> in one. And I will show unto them that fight
> against my word and against my people, who are of
> the House of Israel, that I am God, and that I
> covenanted with Abraham that I would remember
> his seed forever.
> (2 Nephi 29:12–14)

It is unclear exactly who the lost tribes may be today.
History is silent on where those taken into captivity by
the Assyrians later wandered. Jesus Christ, when He visited the Nephites in the Americas after His resurrection,
spoke of being commanded by the Father to minister to
the lost tribes, "for they are not lost unto the Father" (3
Nephi 17:4). Undoubtedly they spread to some extent
around the world, but latter-day prophecies suggest that in

the last days they will be brought forth in some kind of united group and continue to receive divine attention and future blessings. The tenth article of faith of the Church of Jesus Christ of Latter-day Saints states:

> We believe in the literal gathering of Israel and in the Restoration of the Ten Tribes: that Zion (the New Jerusalem) will be built upon the American continent; that Christ will reign personally upon the earth; and, that the earth will be renewed and receive its paradisiacal glory.[6]

The Latter-day Saint concept of the gathering of Israel in the latter days has three aspects: (1) a spiritual gathering, (2) the assembling of church members, as members of the House of Israel, to organized stakes (of Zion) of the church, and (3) the gathering of the descendants of Jacob's twelve sons, including the lost ten tribes, to the lands of their inheritance. The vast majority of these people, obviously, will be other than modern-day Jews.

The spiritual gathering includes coming to know that Jesus is the Christ and joining the Church of Jesus Christ of Latter-day Saints. It will be accomplished by missionaries going forth and seeking out the elect throughout the

---

[6]In passing, one cannot help noting how interesting it is that Maimonides's Thirteen Principles of Faith, mentioned by Rabbi Leffler in chapter 3, has a counterpart in Mormonism's Thirteen Articles of Faith.

world, that is, those receptive to the message brought to them. Some of the people so found will be literal descendants of Jacob/Israel, and others will become so by adoption at baptism. The Book of Mormon and the Doctrine and Covenants are tools to "gather out mine elect" from all the earth (Moses 7:62).

The missionaries of the church are the instruments in the Lord's hand for accomplishing this purpose. The Mormon missionary program began as early as 1830, when missionaries were sent out immediately after the church was founded. Initially, converts "gathered" from the eastern United States, Canada, Britain, and Western Europe. They went first to Ohio, then to Missouri, then to Illinois, and finally to the Great Basin of Utah; but after the beginning of the twentieth century they were no longer asked to immigrate to America and the Salt Lake Valley. Today new converts remain in their own areas or countries and help to build up the church worldwide.

Mormons see the gathering of the Jews to the State of Israel primarily as a political event rather than a spiritual one, but many Latter-day Saints follow events there with particular interest. Orson Hyde's dedicatory prayer in Jerusalem in 1841, petitioning the Lord for the return of "Judah's scattered remnants" to the land of Palestine, makes Mormons the first Zionists, well ahead of the Jewish political Zionists of the late nineteenth century (see the full text of the prayer in Appendix 1).

The return of the Jews in modern times to the "land of their inheritance" is an obvious prerequisite to the fulfillment of biblical prophecies, and some Latter-day Saints (including this writer) feel that the recurrent crises between Israel and her Arab neighbors conform to the prophetic pattern: "For I will gather all nations against Jerusalem to battle," the prophet Zechariah wrote, "and the city shall be taken, and the houses rifled, and the women ravished, and half the city shall go forth into captivity" (Zechariah 14:2). Chapters 12 through 14 of this Hebrew Bible prophet deal with these events and with the coming of the Lord (Messiah) to fight on behalf of the Jews.

Other prophecies relating to the last days of the earth's secular history, as Latter-day Saints interpret them, are to be found, especially in Ezekiel chapters 38 and 39, Joel chapters 2 and 3, and Malachi chapters 3 and 4. Latter-day Saints interpret the eleventh chapter of Isaiah as referring specifically to the gathering of the Jews from the far corners of the earth. These prophecies were given in the language of their times, but those who gave them were looking down the corridors of time to our own era.

All of these prophetic references are subject to interpretation, of course, and most Jews will probably interpret them differently than will most Mormons. There can be no doubt, however, that the political events of the twentieth century, for the first time, at least created the practical and theoretical conditions in the Middle East that are necessary for the Hebrew Bible prophecies to be fulfilled. And these conditions very much concern the House of Israel.

At the end of the nineteenth century, the restoration of the ancient Jewish political state appeared unthinkable, despite Orson Hyde's dedicatory prayer in 1841 for the return of Palestine to the Jews and the nascent Zionist movement of the period. There seemed no realistic way for this to be accomplished. But if God intervenes in history, and this writer believes that He does, then it might well be argued that the twentieth century represents a stupendous example of such divine intervention in order to fulfill His purposes for His Chosen People—the House of Israel.

The events of the twentieth century surely fulfilled the prophecy of Jesus Christ—the Messiah—that the period leading up to His return would be characterized by "wars and rumors of war." In a "revelation and prophecy on war" given through Joseph Smith on December 25, 1832, the Lord declared that "wars . . . will shortly come to pass, beginning with the rebellion in South Carolina. . . . and the time will come that war will be poured out upon all nations, beginning in this place" (Doctrine and Covenants 87:1–2). The American Civil War, which followed, inaugurated the era of modern warfare, involving widespread hardship and devastation to civilian populations.

The rise of virulent nationalism and rampant imperialism reached its apogee in the late nineteenth and early twentieth centuries and climaxed in the two world wars of the first half of the twentieth century. Since the end of World War II it would be difficult to cite a single year in which some form of warfare—international or civil or guerilla—has not been raging in one or more countries

around the world. Unprecedented destruction and geno-
cide characterized this century of conflict.

World War I caused England to issue the Balfour
Declaration, in which Palestine was promised as a home-
land for the Jews. It also destroyed many of the dynasties
of Europe and made possible the rise of both German
Nazism and Soviet Communism, the two most wholly
evil political systems ever to darken the planet. World War
II created the conditions that allowed the Holocaust to
take place, during which six million or more Jews were
murdered by the Nazis. The aftermath led to the mass
migration of Jews to Palestine and the establishment of
the State of Israel in 1948.

Israel was born, however, in the throes of bitter conflict with her Arab neighbors. This first war for Israeli sur-
vival produced a new diaspora, this time of displaced
Palestinian Arabs who either fled or were driven from
their homes. The watershed in the Arab-Israeli conflict
was the 1967 Six-Day War. In less than a week Israel
seized all of Jerusalem from Jordan, the Golan Heights
from Syria in the north, the Sinai desert from Egypt, and
the whole of the West Bank of the Jordan River, previously controlled by Jordan. Although the Sinai was subsequently returned to Egypt after yet another war in 1973,
a large Arab majority continues to live under Israeli juris-
diction in parts of the West Bank (anciently called Judea
and Samaria) and east Jerusalem.

For decades the Mideast "peace process" has been
struggling against the heavy odds of Arab-Israeli antagonism and mutual suspicion. Slow progress has been made

over this period, but many obstacles remain before a true peace is achieved. Jerusalem itself may prove to be the most difficult obstacle. Almost all Israeli Jews, of whatever political persuasion, believe the city should never again be divided. The Arabs, for their part, insist that at least a part of the city must be the capital of their cherished Palestinian state.

The situation is complicated by strong religious feelings on both sides. In the Jewish settlements surrounding Jerusalem and scattered throughout the West Bank in the midst of Arab majorities, there is a very strong feeling that God has restored the ancient state of Israel to its rightful owners and would be displeased if they were now to give it up. On the other side, Arab fundamentalists still seem unreconciled to the permanent existence of any Israeli state.

Thus, the ducks are lined up, so to speak, for the prophecies of Zechariah and other prophets to come to pass. Today Orson Hyde's prayer has been granted; the State of Israel is a reality in what was once called Palestine. But this reality contains the seeds for the possibility of still more warfare in the region, which could theoretically even involve United Nations military intervention (the "all nations" of Zechariah's prophecy?).

Regardless of how the situation may develop in the future, it is likely that most Latter-day Saints will continue to express their perceived religious affinity with the spiritual House of Israel in the form of strong support, as well, for the political State of Israel. We see events taking place there from more than just a political perspective. We see them as the literal fulfillment of prophecy.

We Latter-day Saints often cite the prophet Ezekiel for another reason. Ezekiel 37:16–17 reads:

> Moreover, thou son of man, take thee one stick, and write upon it, for Judah, and for the children of Israel his companions: then take another stick and write upon it, for Joseph, the stick of Ephraim, and for all the house of Israel his companions: And join them one to another into one stick; and they shall become one in thine hand.

For Latter-day Saints, this unification of the sticks of Judah and of Joseph/Ephraim signifies not only a unifying gathering of the whole House of Israel, but also a joining of the Hebrew Bible (the stick of Judah) and the Book of Mormon (the stick of Joseph), since the purpose of the Book of Mormon, as stated on its title page, is to convince "Jew and Gentile that Jesus is the Christ, the Eternal God, manifesting himself unto all nations."

Jacob/Israel's blessing to his son Joseph included these words: "Joseph is a fruitful bough, even a fruitful bough by a well; whose branches run over the wall" (Genesis 49:22). Lehi and his party, who journeyed to the Americas, were all descendants of Joseph, the "fruitful bough" whose "branches run over the wall"—the great ocean.

Patriarchal blessings have already been mentioned. The patriarchal blessing specifically connects each member of the Mormon Church with the House of Israel. Adam was the first patriarch and the father of the human race. He blessed his son Seth, promising that "his posterity should be chosen of the Lord, and that they should be preserved unto the end of the earth" (Doctrine and Covenants 107:42). Abraham, Isaac, and Jacob likewise blessed their children, and Abraham covenanted with God that through his posterity all the families of the earth would be blessed (Genesis 12:1–3). God also promised Abraham and his seed "the blessings of the Gospel, which are the blessings of salvation, even life eternal" (Abraham 2:11). Patriarchal blessings in the Church of Jesus Christ of Latter-day Saints continue this ancient practice.

Two men (or sometimes only one) are usually called at once to be patriarchs in each stake of the church. They are usually older (though not necessarily), spiritually mature high priests, and once they are ordained to this position they hold it for the rest of their lives. The Quorum of the Twelve Apostles has the responsibility of calling and ordaining stake patriarchs "as they shall be designated unto them by revelation" (Doctrine and Covenants 107:39).

Each member of the church is entitled to ask for a patriarchal blessing one time in his or her life. This follows an interview and recommendation from the bishop, based upon the person's readiness and personal worthiness. He or she goes to the patriarch—often to his home—where, under the inspiration of the Holy Ghost, and after fasting and prayer, the patriarch lays his hands on the person's

head and pronounces the blessing. The blessing is recorded and a copy is given to the person receiving it, who
keeps it sacred and may then consult it at any time for
guidance in his or her life.

No two blessings are the same, of course, but all
include a revelation concerning the tribe of Israel from
which the person is descended—back to Abraham. In the
great majority of cases this is through Ephraim, who
received the birthright from Jacob. This could mean either
literally or by adoption (at baptism), but the distinction is
not made. In the case of Lamanites (i.e., natives of the
Western Hemisphere), it may often be through Manasseh,
because the Book of Mormon reveals that Lehi was
descended from Manasseh. Rarely, the blessing may
include lineage from one of the other tribes.

The remainder of the blessing is sometimes in the
form of a prophetic revelation concerning the person's
gifts and talents, and the challenges, callings, and opportunities that may occur throughout the remainder of his or
her life.

A patriarchal blessing does not preempt the right of
every father in the church who holds the Melchizedek
priesthood to give his children a father's blessing. He, too,
is entitled to spiritual inspiration in prophesying to his
sons and daughters, and this may be, in effect, a patriarchal
blessing in its own right.

Sacrifice is a another principle common to both
ancient Israel and Latter-day Saints, although the nature of
the sacrifice is different. When Adam and Eve were driven

from the Garden of Eden they were given the law of sacrifice, whereby they were to offer the firstlings of their
flocks to the Lord (Moses 5:5). Animal, that is, blood, sacrifice, was a feature of Judaism until the destruction of the
Second Temple by the Romans. Mormons understand
that this shedding of blood was in similitude of the future
sacrifice of Jesus Christ for all mankind (Moses 5:7). The
sacrifice of Jesus Christ, as part of the Atonement process,
was to end the practice of sacrifice upon an altar.

Today the law of sacrifice is one of the covenants
made by Latter-day Saints, but it is a willingness to sacrifice all for the building up of the Kingdom of God, and
includes time, talents, and even one's life if necessary. It
also includes the sacrifice of a broken heart, contrite spirit, and daily repentance. In the early days of church history, the Saints willingly sacrificed homes and comforts and
literally their lives for their beliefs. Currently, with that
kind of persecution at least temporarily ended (in some
countries it can still be violent or in the form of social or
family ostracism), sacrifice is likely to take the form of
tithing of one's income and the donation of much time
and talent in service to others, including the missionary
effort to preach the Gospel to all the world, and temple
work for the dead.

The affinity which Latter-day Saints feel for the
ancient House of Israel, and for modern-day Israel and
Jews generally, is thus very broadly based. The similarities
between Moses and Brigham Young, each of whom led
his people in a great exodus from persecution, are strik-

ing. Mormons and Jews share many historic miracles which are memorialized annually. The travails that each people experienced on its journey to the Promised Land forged great spiritual strength. The Scriptures given to both religious societies acknowledge the Lord's hand in their deliverance. Each of us is a covenant people that takes the covenants it has made with God very seriously.

In recent times the Jewish Anti-Defamation League was very helpful in assisting us to overcome local opposition to the construction of temples in Denver and Dallas, an excellent example of Jewish-Mormon cooperation and friendship. With these similarities and affinities very much in mind, the Church of Jesus Christ of Latter-day Saints seeks always to maintain good relations with its Jewish friends, and seeks to accommodate Jewish sensibilities whenever this can be done within the framework of its own revelatory understanding and mission. It respects and honors Judaism and its traditions, so many of which are common to both religions.

Chapter 9

Areas of Misunderstanding and Discussion

This book presents brief portraits of two religions, Mormonism and Judaism, that seldom confront each other with the intention of promoting better understanding between them. More often, books directed to Jews by Mormon authors are intended to convince them of the message of Mormonism so that they will become Mormons. Few, if any, books by Jewish authors try to explain Judaism to Mormons. Hopefully, this book has broken new ground by encouraging a dialogue between these two world religions.

In our effort to consider each of these religions on its own terms, we have presented numerous facets of their respective traditions and practices, each within its own context and approach. Mormonism may have appeared to be more conversionist than Judaism. That is because it is. Judaism may have appeared quite definite about its denial of the messiahship of Jesus. That is because it is. Mormonism seems to have some very specific beliefs. It does. Judaism's belief system seems much more laissez-faire. And it is. Mormonism is quite structured; Judaism less so. Both religions are very family-oriented.

There are significant similarities and differences between the two religions, and we hope that we have covered them adequately. Here we want to review some of them, starting with the similarities because our presentation may not have emphasized them sufficiently.

1. Concern for the integrity of the family and the involvement of all family members in religious activity is an important aspect of both Mormonism and Judaism. Mormonism emphasizes the family with its Monday "Family Home Evening," its belief in the eternal nature of marriage, and its concern for the sanctity of the marriage relationship, especially in sexual matters.

Judaism, as the religion of an historic people, has the family as its basic unit. Many of its religious practices center around the family—the Passover Seder, the B'rit Milah, the intense mourning period, the ceremonies for welcoming the Sabbath, the observance of dietary laws. The Jewish home is apt to have many ritual objects in it—the mezuzah on the doorpost, a Hanukkah menorah, Sabbath candlesticks, to name but a few. It is as filled with religious involvement and observances as the synagogue.

2. For both religions, revelation is not something that occurred only in the distant past, although their views of the nature of God's ongoing revelation are extremely different. Mormonism considers the Book of Mormon and its other sacred texts to be latter-day revelations. In addition, from time to time the president and prophet of the Church proclaims additional revelations as he receives them.

Judaism's tradition of Oral Torah is an extension of God's revelation in Scripture and is ongoing in its attempt to hear and apply the word of God in every human situation, with modern rabbis and teachers continuing to write midrashim (plural of midrash) and halachot (plural of halachah) to enhance the Jew's understanding of how to sanctify life in today's complex world.

3. Both religions foster a sense of community among their adherents.

Mormons feel close to one another and have an elaborate system of support for their co-religionists, with home teaching for families and single members, visiting teaching for women, fast offerings for those in need, priesthood quorums for men, the Relief Society for women, and close social ties among the members.

Judaism, as the religion of an historic people, functions in many "groupy" ways, from the need for a quorum of ten males for a public worship service, to the involvement of family and friends in festive and ritual celebrations, to the many communal organizations that serve the needs of Jews of all persuasions, both religious and secular.

4. Both religions have experienced the antagonism and persecution of other religions or groups over the years.

The early years of the Mormon Church were fraught with angry mobs attacking Mormons and forcing them to move from place to place, until they settled in Utah. Their prophet and founder, Joseph Smith, was murdered by a mob in Illinois. Even today there is strong anti-Mormon sentiment among some people, who openly attack Mormon beliefs in speeches, pamphlets, and films.

Jews have experienced anti-Jewish attacks over the centuries, with many instances of expulsion from their homes and a long history of martyrdom. Historically these incidents occurred because of theological differences, primarily Judaism's denial of the central message of Christianity, the messiahship of Jesus. With the rise of modern nationalism, anti-Judaism became anti-Semitism, based on national and supposed "racial" differences between Jews and other citizens in the countries where they lived, with the most horrendous examples of this occurring during the years of the Nazi Holocaust.

However striking, these similarities cannot mask the significant differences that separate the two religions. More often the differences stand in the way of any ongoing dialogue and bring about misunderstanding and confusion. They are often the source of friction as well.

Perhaps the most obvious place to start in a consideration of these significant differences is with the basic literature of each tradition.

We have already mentioned that the two religions have a body of literature in common. Jews know this literature as the Hebrew Bible. Mormons call it the Old Testament. Many Jews do not regard the Bible as literally true, whereas to Mormonism it is an accurate account of events in the history of the world. Although the Bible may include reliable historical information, Judaism sees the text as also containing myths, legends, the story of God's encounter with His people, and our reaction to this encounter. The Bible includes poetry, fiction, laws, editorializing, and much more. It is primarily a book of religious insight and understanding far beyond the historical narratives.

The differences in how they see the Bible can be a major stumbling block in discussions between adherents of the two religions. When a Jew and a Mormon begin to discuss religion, each of them may assume that the other has the same outlook about the Bible. But this is very much not the case! Mormons generally know very little, if anything, about the rabbinic tradition of biblical interpretation as found in the Oral Torah, a tradition which precludes the kind of biblical literalism that Mormons take for granted. Since the Bible was traditionally thought to be God-given, the rabbis searched each verse of Scripture to learn what insights it contained, often finding more than one lesson, sometimes even conflicting ones, in any given verse. This sort of interpretation is possible in a religion that fosters a both/and outlook on religious teaching. This difference is significant and cannot be overlooked in any meaningful dialogue.

In addition, unlike Mormonism which seeks the "correct" translation, Judaism is not dependent on a translation of the Bible for its insights and lessons. It uses the original Hebrew text. This alone can account for divergent interpretations between Mormons and Jews. A good example would be the passages in the Book of Isaiah that Mormons interpret as referring to Jesus, which Jews totally reject.

The Hebrew text of the Bible was compiled by the Masoretes, a school of scriptural scholars who lived between the sixth and ninth centuries C.E., and who studied every word and letter of the biblical manuscripts available in their day to compile what they considered to be the authentic text. Although many Jewish laypersons are not conversant with Hebrew even today, Jews studying the Bible are almost always guided by a teacher who is, and when questions arise about the precise meaning of the text (as often happens because many Hebrew words have more than one meaning in English), the teacher can return to the original Hebrew to ascertain the nuances of the word under consideration and what its possible meanings may be. This may involve more than one "correct" translation, but that is not a problem. The use of the Hebrew text permits Jewish teachers to gain additional insights by transposing letters in words, spelling them differently, altering their vowels, and juxtaposing them with similar words from other verses elsewhere in the Bible (see Appendix 2 for an example of these techniques). None of this is possible in translation, and therefore is unavailable to Mormon interpreters of the Bible, who rely on the seventeenth-century King James Version.

In addition to the Bible, which it shares with Mormonism, Judaism is also built upon a huge body of postbiblical sacred literature, and since Mormonism has its own collection of postbiblical literature, this represents a major area of difference between the two religions. As indicated earlier, Jewish tradition holds that Moses received two Torahs simultaneously at Mount Sinai, one Written, the other Oral, the latter of which Mormons find very difficult to comprehend as revelation.

The Oral Torah contains the halachic and aggadic traditions with which Judaism interprets the biblical text. It is an extensive literature comprising the Mishnah, the Talmud, the midrashim of the first five centuries after the destruction of the Temple in Jerusalem in the year 70 C.E. by the Romans, as well as all Jewish religious literature since. The Oral Torah functions in the areas of ideas and behavior, as indicated earlier.

Mormonism has no literature of this nature and finds it very confusing indeed. This is especially so because Mormonism believes the Hebrew Bible "to be the word of God as far as it is translated correctly," and also because, unlike Judaism, its tradition of biblical interpretation is based on a translation and not on the Hebrew text. Thus when a Mormon encounters the Oral Torah he does not know what to do with it. He has no "peg" of a similar tradition on which to "hang" his understanding. This difference presented a major stumbling block when I attempted to explain Judaism to Mr. Johnson, especially when I cited ideas based on midrashic literature but not found in the Bible.

As was explained in earlier chapters, the Oral Torah serves as a form of continuing revelation for Jews. However, this kind of revelation is very different from the Mormon concept of modern-day revelation. It is not considered the word of God, as in the Mormon understanding of continuing revelation, but rather is seen as ongoing human insight into what God intends for us to understand from the words of the Written Torah. There is even a passage in the Midrash in which the sages tell God that He no longer has a vote in the matter of interpreting the Torah, since it has been given over into the hands of mankind, a view in marked contrast to what Mormons mean by modern-day revelation.

Later in this chapter Mr. Johnson asks of us Jews, "If God wished to send you a message, how would He get through to you?" This is a Mormon question and not a Jewish one. The comparable Jewish question to the Mormon would be, "How do you know that the message you say you are receiving from God is really from Him and not the product of human invention?"

This is where faith enters in for each religion, and any discussion of the subject is basically unresolvable. As we indicated earlier, Judaism dealt with the question raised by Mr. Johnson sometime after the time of Ezra, when there appeared many prophets with different and often conflicting messages. As a result, Jewish leaders (and we do not know any of the details) decreed that prophecy had ceased in the time of Ezra. For us, then, neither Jesus nor Joseph Smith can be considered a prophet in the biblical sense of the word. They came along too late. Here is another major source of misunderstanding between the two religions.

A further aspect of the difficulty with the use of Hebrew Scriptures is that Mormonism tends to take the historical parts of the Bible literally, sometimes viewing them from the perspective of what is stated in their post-biblical Mormon literature. This may lead to very different interpretations of the same passage, and oftentimes one tradition will see no theological meaning in a passage that the other finds cogent or even crucial.

Related to the problems deriving from our views on the literal accuracy of the Bible, Mr. Johnson and I also differed about modern biblical criticism. As a Jew I am able to accept the prevailing scholarship in our time that analyzes the Hebrew Bible and the Christian New Testament as products of human editing and interpretation. Mr. Johnson, as a Mormon, discounts these efforts (as the reader will note later in this chapter) with the comment that these scholars often disagree with one another, and that the authors of the Bible lived much closer in time to the events about which they were writing and thus the text they produced should be accepted as written.

It appeared to me that Mormon theological presuppositions prevented Mr. Johnson from considering the text as anything other than revelation. He seemed to be married to the text *qua* text, unable to see it as the product of human authors and editors, all of them writing in specific times and places, with a preconceived agenda that colored what they included and what they excluded; in short, that the Bible was not produced in an historical vacuum.

Mr. Johnson's comments later in this chapter about the efforts of two Jewish scholars to place the crucifixion in an historical context reflect the Mormon difficulty with historical theory. Even if a hypothetical reconstruction seems plausible, he rejects it if not in accordance with revelation. As in so many other aspects of the discussion that led to this book, revelation superseded scholarship for him whenever scholarship raised questions about the passages under consideration.

Mr. Johnson's either/or outlook often surfaced in our correspondence. In our discussions of this, I realized that I took a both/and outlook. We Jews do not hold to an absolutist view of truth, and as Mr. Johnson points out at the beginning of his part of this concluding chapter, Mormonism does. We are able to find many truths in a text, utilizing them when appropriate, setting them aside when they do not seem appropriate. And halachah is often situational in its decision of an ethical problem, as the passage in Appendix 3 dealing with sterilization of the feebleminded indicates. Judaism is not absolutist either in belief or in its approach to ethics. Here is another significant difference between the two religions, and one that can be another stumbling block in understanding between them.

A second major area of misunderstanding arises around the role of the Messiah. The belief in a future person (the word Messiah literally means "anointed one") who will come and redeem the world from war and human strife was initially a Jewish belief. It is not inherently found in the biblical text but is dependent on the proof-text method developed by the Pharisees, which brings together numerous texts from different places in Scripture in order to develop a new idea.

Using this method to interpret the Bible, Judaism sees the Messiah as a human being (not a God incarnate), traditionally believed to be a literal descendant of King David, who will come and redeem the world from war and strife. As we Jews look at the world, such a person has yet to come. The world is not redeemed. It is still full of human suffering and agony, and no amount of faith in a supposed Messiah who has already come can belie that. Thus Jews still wait for God to bring the Messiah or the messianic age, even though Mr. Johnson faults us for not having produced a Messiah as yet. But for us, this decision is God's, and not for us to bring about.

However, there were people in the past who proclaimed themselves to be the Messiah without this worldwide transformation having taken place. We call them false Messiahs and would put Jesus in this category, as we do with the others who proclaimed themselves or were proclaimed to be the Messiah.

Another significant difference between Judaism and Christianity, and Mormonism specifically, is the atoning role of Jesus for human sin.

Judaism does not have a doctrine of vicarious atonement in which someone can atone for the sins of another person. We believe that everyone must atone for his own sins. The holiday of Yom Kippur, the Day of Atonement, focuses on this process on two levels—sins between a human being and his fellow human beings, and sins between the individual and God.

For the former, Judaism teaches that when there is sin between human beings, atonement can only occur after the sinner has sought the forgiveness of those against whom he has sinned; then can he seek God's forgiveness. However, if the sin is against God and does not involve another person, then he can go directly to God for forgiveness.

Thus Mormonism's assertion that Jesus's death atoned for the sins of all people presents a major stumbling block for the Jew. We do not believe that anyone can atone for another person's sin, and especially not as the fulfillment of any biblical teaching, or the Law of Moses, as Mormons term it.

For the Christian, belief in the Messiah became a core belief, as witnessed by the very name "Christian," and Mormonism affirms this belief. By contrast, in Judaism the hope for the coming of the Messiah is one of many religious ideas, but certainly is not central in the same way. Thus something that is a major focus in Mormonism is of lesser concern for Jews. This is not to denigrate the Christian belief but merely to emphasize that there is a significant difference between the two religions in respect to the role of the Messiah. This difference often presents a problem in interreligious understanding, especially since Christianity is meaningless without Jesus as the Messiah and Judaism does not need to focus on this belief in order to exist.

An additional point of difference, and one that neither of us considered prior to our completion of this book, is the title we selected for it. The notion of two Houses of Israel is a problem for both Jews and Mormons.

Historically, there is only one House of Israel, the Jews. We are linear descendants (plus converts) of the people of the Bible. Our history can be traced through the biblical period and up to the present day. On the other hand, Mormons also consider themselves to be of the House of Israel, as Mr. Johnson indicates in chapter 8. This is a Mormon theological statement which Jews reject. Even the use of this term can be a stumbling block in dialogue.

And again I would emphasize that the difference between the either/or outlook of Mormonism and the both/and outlook of Judaism can also be a major problem in dialogue. Mr. Johnson emphasizes the Mormon outlook in his section of this chapter. Jews do not feel the need to take such an approach to our religion, whether in the historical literature, in the lessons we learn from Scripture, or in our consideration of ethical questions. We can easily encompass more than one understanding of a subject without setting up the true/false or right/wrong dichotomy that Mr. Johnson presents.

Still, perhaps the most obvious difficulty in any dialogue between the two religions is Mormonism's emphasis on converting non-Mormons to Mormonism. Jews do not feel the need to convert non-Jews to Judaism, and are befuddled by such efforts and resent them when they are directed at themselves. Jews believe that their religion is quite complete without the addition of Christian beliefs, whether of a more traditional kind or as formulated by Mormonism. Jews also take great umbrage when their religion is denigrated by conversionists who imply that they have the truth and that the beliefs of non-Mormons are somehow of lesser merit. Jews resent such behavior whenever it is directed at them or at deceased Jews, as it was when Mormons attempted to baptize by proxy the martyrs of the Holocaust. Here is another stumbling block in promoting understanding between the two religions.

These various differences are significant. They can very well pose serious problems in interreligious dialogue between Mormonism and Judaism. But if dialogue is to occur, then both sides must look honestly at their differences, for the similarities are never a problem. And while the differences may be distressing, understanding them is crucial to a successful dialogue, in which each participant knows what his tradition has to say in the many areas under consideration and has respect for the other party's views. Further, it is crucial that both sides in the dialogue begin from the premise that they are not out to convert the other. Only on that basis can there be the kind of forthright discussion that will lead to improved understanding. Nonetheless marked conflict and disagreement will remain in spite of the best intentions of both groups to bridge them.

Rabbi William J. Leffler

In this concluding chapter, Rabbi Leffler has well summarized the similarities between Judaism and Mormonism. There is much that unites our two religions and should draw us together. These common features can serve as a basis for a better understanding and improved relationship between us.

Mormons strongly desire such an improvement. We believe in the core of Judaism. Jewish talk-show host Dennis Prager states: "God is the source of morality in Judaism."[1] We Mormons declare equally that God is the source of morality in Mormonism. What could be more core than this at a time when much of the world openly declares that man, not God, is and should be the only source of whatever morality still exists? Both religions teach and believe in the highest standards of ethical conduct. For us, Jesus' teachings expanded upon, and did not refute, the teachings of Judaism. As discussed in the preceding chapter, we Mormons consider ourselves to be brothers and sisters to our Jewish friends. We are unique among Christians in that sense.

Nevertheless, some of the differences between us are indeed important (although others are not), and Rabbi Leffler has well summarized them from the Jewish perspective. They now require comment from the Mormon side.

Each of us has touched upon the words "true" and "truth" in our presentation or discussion. It became

---

[1]*Moment* magazine, June 1999.

apparent in our early correspondence that we understand these words differently as they apply to religious history and divine commandment. It was a significant stumbling block between us as we sought to understand each other's religious beliefs.

Mormons regard truth in an absolute sense. For most Jews, truth is largely relative. Most Jews are not doctrinaire or absolutist either in their religious beliefs or their moral teachings, although it is worth noting that there are some who are—especially the more traditionalist ones. On the other hand, most Mormons tend to be so in both areas. But for Mormons our absolutism comes directly from God, and so it is not subject to scholarly interpretation or debate. Neither can we expect to be able to reject these moral absolutes without consequences, both in this world and in the next.

The essence of Mormon doctrine is that God has revealed to us specific answers to many of the most fundamental questions about the purpose of earth life and how it relates to each individual's pre-mortal and post-mortal condition. We do not claim to have all the answers, but we rejoice in those which we have received through the Book of Mormon and other latter-day revelation. Because we have been given these answers in a very special way, we wish to share them with others. We do not do this out of any sense of smugness or superiority, but because we sincerely believe that what we have to offer to the world will contribute to the well-being and happiness of our fellow humans, both in this life and the next.

We believe that we can know God only as He chooses to reveal Himself, and that His method for doing so is
to call prophets. Religion, any religion, is not a matter of
proof, but of faith. To prove is to force men to believe. We
do not believe that God acts in this way, and neither do
we attempt to *prove* anything to anyone. Nor do we
Latter-day Saints attempt to force our religion or beliefs
upon anyone. God calls prophets and endows them with
priesthood power, so that for those with sufficient *faith* to
accept them, "evidences" can be provided that will testify
that the prophet speaks with the revelatory authority of
God Himself (e.g., the miracles performed by Moses during the Exodus). So it was with the prophets of the
Hebrew Bible, whom the ancient Jews recognized and
accepted as such, and so we claim for Joseph Smith as a
prophet of God, and for the Book of Mormon as a second witness to the divine messiahship of Jesus of
Nazareth. We make these claims as simple declarative
statements of fact. For us they are true. We present evidences for these statements of fact, for these truths as we
have received them. Let others, including Jews, accept or
reject them as they will.

A few examples of simple logic may better illustrate
the message that we offer to the world. The Book of
Mormon is either an ancient document translated by
Joseph Smith or it is a nineteenth-century document
written by him or some other, unknown author. It may
also be "interesting religious literature," as Rabbi Leffler
commented to me after reading it, but there is no third

choice as to its historicity. In that sense it is either true that it is an ancient document or else the claim is false. Mormons affirm that it is true and ask others to read it and judge for themselves. The Book of Mormon itself serves as the best evidence for its own authenticity.

Likewise, if God exists—and both Mormons and Jews agree that He does—He must be either corporeal or incorporeal; He cannot be both. Mormons assert that God the Father is corporeal not only because the Hebrew for "image" and "likeness" in Genesis 1:26 permits the interpretation that God *looks* like us (as Rabbi Leffler conceded to me) but because He has revealed through a modern prophet, Joseph Smith, that He has a physical body of flesh and bone. Each person must judge for himself/herself whether Joseph's story of his initial Vision— the appearance before him of the Father and the Son as two distinct personages—and later revelation, that the Father has a body of flesh and bone, are credible.

To carry the point even further, God either is what He is independent of human reasoning, in which case there is only one true God, or else He is whatever men may imagine or desire Him to be, in which case there are many true Gods. There is either one true religion or else all religions are equally true (or false). Jesus of Nazareth was and is the divine Son of God, the Messiah, or He was not and is not. And so on.

Rabbi Leffler takes issue with these Mormon either/ors because they conflict with the both/and of Judaism, which he explains as meaning that a passage of

Scripture (or an ethical/moral question) can have *both* one meaning *and* another meaning that is in conflict with it, but that both can be acceptable. That may be in the case of biblical exegesis, but there is a point, as with the questions cited above, at which logic takes over and allows *only* an either/or conclusion. There is no way to answer any of these questions definitively unless God reveals the answers to us. Mormons affirm that He has done so.

For all of the reasons cited by Rabbi Leffler, Jews are dismayed and sometimes angered by these affirmations, including our perceived connection with the House of Israel, which they reject and which Rabbi Leffler regards as "traditional Mormon polemics regarding Judaism." Regrettably from the Mormon standpoint, most Jews will not read the Book of Mormon, or any other Mormon Scripture, and put it to their own personal test, in part because they reject it on *a priori* grounds. *A priori* in this case means to reject the Book of Mormon, or any other text, for *prior* reasons, such as Jewish traditions, unrelated to the text itself. By this form of reasoning the Book of Mormon is not true because it *cannot* be. And it cannot be true, in Jewish opinion, because it tells of the appearance of Jesus Christ to the ancient inhabitants of the Americas after His crucifixion in Jerusalem, thus confirming His divinity as the Son of God and as the prophesied Messiah.

Although the question of the Messiah is not central to Jewish religious concerns, it lies at the heart of our differences. One might almost say that all the other differences between us are merely over details. For example, Mr.

Prager also states in *Moment* that "Judaism affirms the afterlife." So do all Mormons. He also worries about "the widespread acceptance of abortion as a form of birth control." So do almost all Mormons. The latter may be only Prager's personal opinion, but it is refreshing to learn the viewpoint of one prominent Jewish spokesman on such a controversial question.

Most Christians, and all Latter-day Saint Christians, however, accept Jesus as the foretold Messiah of the Hebrew Bible. The New Testament declares that Jesus was, in fact, a descendant of King David. Many of Jesus' Jewish contemporaries who were closely associated with Him accepted Him as the Messiah also, and were among the first Christians. Today, Judaism avers that a Jew may not accept Jesus as the Messiah and still remain a Jew. Although he may still consider himself to be a Jew, in the eyes of other Jews he has converted to another religion, namely Christianity, and forsaken Judaism.

We Latter-day Saints regret the Jewish rejection of Jesus as the Messiah. However, from a Christian perspective, it was necessary that the Jewish political leadership of that day should scorn Jesus and demand that the Romans crucify Him. Otherwise, the atoning sacrifice (for the sins of all men), which included Jesus' physical sacrifice as the fulfillment of the law of Moses, could not have taken place, and His divine mission as Redeemer of the world could not have been fully completed. After his atonement and resurrection, Jesus declared to the people in the New World: "The law is fulfilled that was given unto Moses.

Behold, I am he that gave the law, and I am he who covenanted with my people Israel" (3 Nephi 15:4–9).

We also note, in response to Judaism's denial of Jesus, that for Jews God has so far failed to produce an accepted Messiah or messianic age. As Rabbi Leffler points out in an earlier chapter, the concept in many Jewish minds has changed from belief in a personal Messiah to belief in a messianic age when there will be universal peace and well-being. Nonetheless, those Jews who still believe in a personal Messiah believe that he will be a purely human person who in some manner will bring this about. Mormons believe that this is a misunderstanding of the prophesied nature and role of the Messiah. The universal peace that Jews are expecting from a Messiah will occur after His second appearance.

There are many references to this Second Coming in both the Old and New Testaments. Isaiah chapter 53 (as Mormons understand it) is perhaps the most explicit reference in the Hebrew Bible regarding the Messiah's first appearance, whereas Zechariah chapters 12–14 most plainly prophesy about the events and circumstances of His Second Coming. Joel and Daniel also address the subject. In the New Testament Jesus speaks of the time of His return to earth in the twenty-fourth chapter of Matthew, and the apostle John receives a great revelation (the Book of Revelation) on the island of Patmos concerning the same climactic battle for Jerusalem that was revealed to Zechariah. It is at the very moment of utter desperation for the Jewish defenders of the city that Jesus the Messiah will come again, this time as the Conquering Messiah who will defeat their enemies in battle and be finally recognized by His Chosen People for who He was and is. This will then truly usher in the messianic age.

So, while all Mormons and many Jews still believe in the coming of a Messiah, Jews expect that it will be the first time only, and he will be entirely human; for us it will be the second time, and He will be Jesus Christ, the Son of God.

From the discussion in this chapter as well as preceding ones, it is evident that the question of revelation constitutes another of the significant differences between us. For Mormons, it is at our core; we believe in continuing revelation from God through modern prophets. For Jews, the idea of revelation as Mormons understand it appears so hypothetical as to be meaningless; the last recognized Jewish prophet was in the time of Ezra, who lived more than four hundred years before the birth of Jesus. Thus, while God may send a Messiah in his own good time, He is not allowed by the Jews to send any more prophets— either to the Jews or anyone else. Therefore the Mormon might ask of the Jew, "If God wished to send you a message, how would He get through to you?"

Rabbi Leffler's answer earlier in this chapter is very Jewish: "It is not a Jewish question."

It is also very Jewish to answer a question with another question. He asks of me, "How do you know that the message you say you are receiving from God is really from Him and not the product of human invention?"

This is a very fair question, but one that can also be

answered—in the Jewish fashion—with another question: "How do Jews know that the words of those whom they did and still do recognize as prophets anciently were actually from God and not the product of human invention?" Why did Saul fear the prophet Samuel's warning that he had condemned himself for failing to follow the commands of the Lord? Why did David accept the condemnation of the prophet Nathan because of his adultery with Bathsheba and the murder of her husband? Although these men were kings, they recognized and bowed before the words of a prophet.

Rabbi Leffler's question also deserves a more direct answer. How do Mormons know, how can anyone truly *know*, that a man is a prophet, and that when he speaks as such, he speaks as the mouthpiece of the Lord? The answers are simple: (1) one must first have an open mind, (2) one must ask of God, that is, pray for an answer, (3) one must have faith that he will receive an answer, and (4) one must not be afraid to receive the answer.

All spiritual knowledge comes through this step-by-step process. It is the process by which Mormons can genuinely state that they know that Joseph Smith was a prophet of God, that the church which he established is the authentic church upon the earth today, and that the current president of the church, Gordon B. Hinckley, is a living prophet on the earth today.

The work of a Hebrew prophet was to act as God's messenger and make known God's will. It was also the prophet's duty to denounce sin and foretell its punishment. He was to be, above all, a preacher of righteousness.

When the people had fallen away from a true faith in Jehovah, the prophets had to try and restore that faith and remove false views about the character of God and the nature of the Divine requirement.

The role of the president/prophets of the Church of Jesus Christ of Latter-day Saints in modern times is very similar to this ancient prophetic role. Beginning with the calling of the boy Joseph Smith in 1820 as the first prophet of the Restoration, God has revealed to the whole world—if it will but hearken to His voice—His mind and will, as He did anciently to His Chosen People, the House of Israel. As evidences of this fact, "miracles" of all kinds abound, the most important of these being the bringing forth of the Book of Mormon, the record of God's dealing with one group of ancient Americans, descendants of the House of Israel in the New World.

Rabbi Leffler is quite correct, however, in stating the role that faith must play in recognizing a true prophet of God. When there is faith the miracle follows; it is seldom the other way around (Saul's experience on the road to Damascus might be considered an exception). When the boy prophet Joseph Smith went out into the woods near his home to pray that spring morning in 1820, he had the faith to believe that his prayer would be answered. And so it was, as both God the Father and Jesus Christ the Son appeared before him—a sublime miracle which he could in no way doubt or deny.

It is the same principle by which personal revelation comes into play for Mormons. We know that the Book of Mormon is true and that Joseph Smith was a prophet of

God less by "rational" analysis—although that too can play a role—than by the exercise of faith in Christ. The Holy Ghost then confirms those truths to us. That is the basis of the missionary discussions which we present to investigators.

Jews will understandably find this process difficult to follow. There is nothing similar to it in their tradition. Mormons perceive Judaism as a highly intellectualized religion, recognizing and accepting, as it does, many differing opinions concerning belief and behavior. Although Rabbi Leffler, and Jews in general, consider the Oral Torah to be a form of ongoing revelation, Latter-day Saints would have difficulty in applying that definition to it. We respect the Oral Torah as a guideline for Jews who can no longer accept revelation through prophets in the classical sense that we do, but we do not believe that the nature and the will of God are subject to discovery by the unaided intellect, no matter how learned or brilliant.

The twelfth-century Jewish philosopher and scholar Maimonides, for example, reflecting traditional Jewish belief, asserted that God cannot be corporeal because God is perfect, and a perfect being could not have a physical, and thus corruptible, body. This may appear to be a reasonable intellectual conclusion, although it might also be argued that a formless, infinite, unembodied God is more difficult for the human, finite mind to comprehend than a corporeal one. Mormons, on the other hand, assert that God the Father appeared to the boy prophet Joseph Smith as a physical being, and that He has otherwise revealed that He has an incorruptible and perfected body of flesh and bone, just as all resurrected beings will have. For Mormons such direct revelations supersede all intellectual arguments to the contrary.

Along the same lines, Mormons reject purely scholastic challenges or debates concerning the authority or accuracy of the Scriptures, for these represent the intellectual conclusions of men, which often differ. Intellectual knowledge is important to us, and members are urged to seek such knowledge, but we recognize its limitations in the realm of religious truth. While we respect scholarship in general, including biblical scholarship, the scholars were not present and can have no direct knowledge of what actually took place.

Rabbi Leffler has referred in his portion of this chapter to the differences we discovered in our respective approaches to revelation as it may be contradicted by scholarship. The example he cites may be illustrative.

In the course of our correspondence, a debate arose between us over the question of who/what crucified Christ. As a Jew, Rabbi Leffler is understandably disinclined to accept the Gospel accounts of the crucifixion and resurrection of Jesus at face value. He regards these accounts as "Christian propaganda," to use his characterization. We decided to submit the question to the test of biblical scholarship.

Rabbi Leffler asked me to read the works of two Jewish scholars—experts on the period of the Roman occupation of Judea during the time of Jesus. In turn, I asked him to read a work by a renowned Mormon scholar of the same period. Predictably, each of us found the other's scholarship unsatisfactory, affected by the respective biases and presuppositions of the scholars, that is, that Jesus either was or was not the Messiah. The Jewish scholars could not accept the possibility that the Gospel accounts of the crucifixion could be accurate and still remain Jews (a very significant impediment). The Mormon scholar, naturally, based his scholarship on the opposite presupposition that the Gospel writers got it generally right concerning the circumstances of Jesus' crucifixion, whatever differences there might be in detail.

Each of the Jewish scholars offered alternative, and conflicting, arguments for the proposition that the Roman procurator, Pontius Pilate, willingly condemned Jesus to death, and not reluctantly under the prodding of the Jewish religious leaders, as the Gospel writers tell the story.

One of them suggested that Jesus was a purely religious "charismatic of charismatics" whose misfortune it was that he attracted crowds—something that Pilate particularly feared because it might lead to anti-Roman demonstrations. In the view of this scholar this sealed Jesus' fate. His death was thus a preemptive, entirely Roman execution, supported by Jewish leaders who owed their positions to Rome and who likewise feared the possibility of crowds getting out of control.

The other scholar argued, in contrast, that Jesus was primarily an anti-Roman political revolutionary and executed as such. The only historical evidence of this, he conceded, was the title hung around Jesus' neck ("Jesus of Nazareth King of the Jews"). He based his conclusion on this single fact.

Although I conceded that the first theory was plausible, it did not convince me. On purely objective, intellectual grounds, as I explained to Rabbi Leffler, I find the Gospel accounts of the crucifixion at least equally as plausible as the theories advanced by the Jewish scholars. Scholarship may offer alternative explanations to revelation, but not necessarily superior ones. The Gospel accounts of the crucifixion are no less reasonable than the various scholarly alternatives unless one's presuppositions (or desire to remain a Jew) rule them out on the grounds that they are not valid because they cannot be valid (*a priori* logic).

The twentieth-century scholars were most certainly not there, so how can any of them know *for sure?* Pontius Pilate was there, but he left no memoirs to tell us what really happened. The Book of Mormon testifies that the resurrected Christ visited the people of the Western Hemisphere. This is revelation for Mormons which serves as a second witness to the Bible that Jesus of Nazareth was and is the Messiah, the divine Son of God. It thus verifies for us the Gospel accounts and renders moot alternative scholarly *theories.*

Mormons accept the Bible as literally accurate Scripture as far as it is translated correctly, but where the Bible is unclear or ambiguous, as it often is (i.e., the many acceptable, yet differing, translations from Hebrew into

English), or when biblical scholarship contradicts revelation, as it often does, the Book of Mormon and other modern-day revelations take precedence. For Mormons, these clarify and restore to the Scriptures much of what has been lost or altered by scribal error as they were copied and edited, or deliberately removed as they passed through the hands of uninspired men.

As Rabbi Leffler indicates, a major point of friction between the two religions is likely to result from the strong missionary effort of the Church of Jesus Christ of Latter-day Saints. Mormons do not target Jews in our missionary efforts, but neither do we exclude them as they seem to wish us to do. Many Jews such as Rabbi Leffler resent the inclusion of Jews in our missionary program and understandably ask why.

I attempt to answer this question in chapter 6, "Mormonism in Practice," but the reader needs a fuller explanation in this summation. It begins with the Book of Mormon.

The Book of Mormon is the keystone of Mormonism. It was written on the American continent by Jewish prophets and their descendants who wrote for the Jews of our times as much as for the Gentiles. It contains an account of the appearance of Jesus the Messiah to these people in the Western Hemisphere after His crucifixion in Jerusalem. It was thus written, as Mormon states in the frontispiece, "To the convincing of the Jew and Gentile that Jesus is the Christ, the Eternal God, manifesting himself unto all nations."

Mormons understand that Jews, *speaking collectively,* do not accept or believe the Book of Mormon to be true in the sense that we use that word. But we consider that this rejection is not necessarily set in stone and does not necessarily apply to all Jews, some of whom do believe the Book of Mormon to be true and have accepted the message of the missionaries and have joined the church. Mormons accept the Book of Mormon and believe it to be true both historically and in its revelatory religious message to *all* people in these latter days. Should it be any wonder, then, that we Latter-day Saints, as bearers of this prophetic record, understand that our mission involves carrying this message to *both* Jews and Gentiles?

Latter-day Saints strongly believe that all people, everywhere, should be free to hear, and either accept or reject, the message of the Book of Mormon and the Restoration. In a few countries, the lack of religious freedom still precludes our missionaries from entering. Worldwide, this exclusion seems to be gradually ending. In the case of Jews, it is difficult for us to understand why the accident of Jewish birth, as Jews might consider it (because they do not generally believe in a spirit pre-existence prior to birth), should necessarily preclude a person from the right to hear, and then accept or reject, what we have to tell him or her.

In our correspondence, Rabbi Leffler declared that a Jew who converts to Mormonism or any form of Christianity is a traitor, presumably to his Jewish heritage, who deserves what he gets, meaning the anger and social ostracism from fellow Jews that often follow such conversions. This seems unduly harsh. It seems to us that when such a conversion occurs, the individual Jew who thus accepts the basic tenets of another religion should be granted the right to freely make such a choice when he determines that such tenets are correct, or *true for him*, and then be left in peace accordingly. This is freedom of religion in practice.

Nevertheless, we Mormons need to be more sensitive to the feelings of our Jewish friends in this regard. What came out of the correspondence between Rabbi Leffler and myself is perhaps a realization that there are two fundamental principles in conflict here, each of which is legitimate in its own context.

As Rabbi Leffler has explained in this book, by virtue of his birth a Jew becomes part of an historic people—the Jewish people. He may or may not accept Judaism in whole or in part as a *religion*, as he pleases, but he is not free to betray—as Jews see it—his historic heritage, his people. By doing so he is also betraying, in the Jewish view, the covenant which Israel—and by implication he himself—made with God at Sinai.

This principle overrides, for Jews, the equally valid principle for us Mormons, which is freedom of conscience, freedom to choose, or as we call it, (free) agency. This, it seems to me, is the nub of the misunderstanding that arises between us concerning our missionary effort as it may affect Jews.

We do understand that Jews, as a whole, say, "Leave us alone!" when we bring them our message. But missionary work is done one-on-one. When any individual, Jew or non-Jew, tells our missionaries to depart, they will respect this wish and immediately comply. The person will be left alone. But as long as even one Jew, anywhere, says, "Tell me more" and is willing to listen, as is sometimes the case, he or she will be taught, and if they so desire, will be baptized and confirmed as a member of the church.

We Latter-day Saints could not do otherwise and still remain true to our own deeply held religious beliefs, including the principle of free agency. If we exclude Jews from our missionary effort, we would be traitors to those beliefs and teachings in no less a way than Jews consider to be traitors those of their number who accept those teachings. This is the honest difference of principle that necessarily leaves Jews and Mormons at an impasse. And I agree with Rabbi Leffler that it is not a "detail" that separates us on this point.

We do (or should) understand that Jewish conversions to Mormonism will be unsettling to other Jews, who will thereafter reject the person who converted as a Jew. This is unfortunate, but not too dissimilar from the experiences of many early Gentile converts, who also sometimes had to face rejection by their family and friends as a consequence of joining the church. While such rejection was more common in the nineteenth century, it still happens today. We would only ask our Jewish friends to consider the possibility that a few of their number might wish to have their ultimate questions considering the reason for their existence answered by something more than another question. The diversity of human nature is such that even some Jews may come to prefer a religion that offers definition to one that studiously does not.

Of course, sometimes the shoe could be on the other foot. Mormons see their children or friends leave the church for any number of reasons. We are sad when this happens, but we are seldom angry with them. They have not broken an historic continuity as the Jew does when he becomes a Mormon. In our case we try to win back those who leave the church. But ultimately, we recognize their freedom to choose for themselves. This is their God-given right. We love them nonetheless.

A major purpose of this book, therefore, from my perspective as a Mormon, is to try to explain to the Jewish reader why Mormons are who we are, and why we do what we do from a proselytizing standpoint. We have no quarrel with modern Judaism, for we very much associate ourselves with the beliefs and practices of ancient Judaism. This may cause Jews to have a quarrel with us, since they reject such an association, but we are merely stating our own religious beliefs and understandings, not arguing with or denigrating theirs. We do not wish to be polemical, but it is virtually impossible for us to explain our beliefs without being "conversionist." We do not intend for this to be a point of friction, but we understand why it may be. It is the clash between the Mormon belief that all men and women should be fully free to hear what God has revealed through modern-day prophets, versus the strongly held Jewish belief that Judaism is complete within itself and that this message is not for them.

Although these two contradictory beliefs/understand-ings/outlooks may never be fully reconciled during our mortal lives, I hope that our Jewish friends will under-stand and appreciate the respect and love that Mormons have for them. As a persecuted people ourselves, we understand and sympathize with the long Jewish history of persecution by their Christian enemies, a history which we deplore. We do not believe that God loves the Jews any less than any of His other children. Jews remain His Chosen People, and we Mormons consider that we are also members of the House of Israel. Our modern revela-tion does not deny Judaism but only expands upon it. Yes, we have differences. Nevertheless, I hope that what we have in common will always prevail over what divides us; for surely we are all children of the same God.

Frank J. Johnson

Appendix 1

Prayer of Orson Hyde
on the Mount of Olives
October 24, 1841

O Thou! Who art from everlasting to everlasting, eternally and unchangeably the same, even God who rules in the heavens above, and controls the destinies of men on earth, wilt Thou not condescend, through Thine infinite goodness and royal favor, to listen to the prayer of Thy servant which he this day offers up unto Thee in the name of Thy holy child Jesus, upon this land, where the Sun of Righteousness set in blood, and thine Anointed One expired.

Be pleased, O Lord, to forgive all follies, weaknesses, vanities, and sins of Thy servant, and strengthen him to resist all future temptations. Give him prudence and discernment that he may avoid the evil and choose the good; give him fortitude to bear up under trying and adverse circumstances, and grace to endure all things for Thy name's sake, until the end shall come, when all the Saints shall rest in peace.

Now, O Lord! Thy servant has been obedient to the heavenly vision which Thou gavest him in his native land;

and under the shadow of Thine outstretched arm, he has
safely arrived in this place to dedicate and consecrate this
land unto Thee, for the gathering together of Judah's scattered remnants, according to the predictions of the holy
Prophets—for the building up of Jerusalem again after it
has been trodden down by the Gentiles so long, and for
rearing a Temple in honor of Thy name. Everlasting
thanks be ascribed to Thee, O Father, Lord of heaven and
earth, that Thou hast preserved Thy servant from the dan-
gers of the seas, and from the plague and pestilence which
have caused the land to mourn. The violence of man has
also been restrained, and Thy providential care by night
and by day has been exercised over Thine unworthy servant. Accept, therefore, O Lord, the tribute of a grateful
heart for all past favors, and be pleased to continue Thy
kindness and mercy towards a needy worm of the dust.

O Thou, Who didst covenant with Abraham, Thy
friend, and Who didst renew that covenant with Isaac, and
confirm the same with Jacob with an oath, that Thou
wouldst not only give them this land for an everlasting
inheritance, but that Thou wouldst also remember their
seed forever. Abraham, Isaac, and Jacob have long since
closed their eyes in death, and made the grave their man-
sion. Their children are scattered and disbursed abroad
among the nations of the Gentiles like sheep that have no
shepherd, and are still looking forward for the fulfillment
of those promises which Thou didst make concerning
them; and even this land, which once poured forth
nature's richest bounty, and flowed as it were, with milk

and honey, has, to a certain extent, been smitten with barrenness and sterility since it drank from murderous hands the blood of Him who never sinned.

Grant, therefore, O Lord, in the name of Thy wellbeloved Son, Jesus Christ, to remove the barrenness and sterility of this land, and let springs of living water break forth to water its thirsty soil. Let the vine and olive produce in their strength, and the fig tree bloom and flourish. Let the land become abundantly fruitful when possessed by its rightful heirs; let it again flow with plenty to feed the returning prodigals who come home with a spirit of grace and supplication; upon it let the clouds distill virtue and richness, and let the fields smile with plenty. Let the flocks and the herds greatly increase and multiply upon the mountains and the hills; and let Thy great kindness conquer and subdue the unbelief of Thy people. Do thou take from them their stony heart, and give them a heart of flesh; and may the Sun of Thy favor dispel the cold mists of darkness which have beclouded their atmosphere. Incline them to gather in upon this land according to Thy word. Let them come like clouds and like doves to their windows. Let the large ships of the nations bring them from the distant isles; and let kings become their nursing fathers, and queens with motherly fondness wipe the tear of sorrow from their eye.

Thou, O Lord, did once move upon the heart of Cyrus to show favor unto Jerusalem and her children. Do Thou now also be pleased to inspire the hearts of kings and the powers of the earth to look with a friendly eye toward this place, and with a desire to see Thy righteous purposes executed in relation thereto. Let them know that it is Thy good pleasure to restore the kingdom unto Israel—raise up Jerusalem as its capital, and constitute her people a distinct nation and government, with David Thy servant, even a descendant from the loins of ancient David to be their king.

Let that nation or that people who shall take an active part on behalf of Abraham's children, and in the raising up of Jerusalem, find favor in Thy sight. Let not their enemies prevail against them, neither let pestilence or famine overcome them, but let the glory of Israel overshadow them, and the power of the Highest protect them; while that nation or kingdom which will not serve Thee in this glorious work must perish, according to Thy word—"Yea, those nations shall be utterly wasted."

Though Thy servant is now far from his home, and the land bedewed with his earliest tear, yet he remembers, O Lord, his friends who are there, and family, whom for Thy sake he has left. Though poverty and privation be our earthly lot, yet ah! Do Thou richly endow us with an inheritance where moth and rust do not corrupt, and where thieves do not break through and steal.

The lands that have fed, clothed, or shown favor unto the family of Thy servant in his absence, or that shall hereafter do so, let them not lose their reward, but let a special blessing rest upon them, and in Thy kingdom let them have an inheritance when Thou shalt come to be glorified in this society.

Do Thou also look with favor upon all those through whose liberality I have been enabled to come to this land; and in the day when Thou shalt reward all people according to their works, let those also not be passed by or forgotten, but in time let them be in readiness to enjoy the glory of those mansions which Jesus has gone to prepare. Particularly do Thou bless the stranger in Philadelphia, whom I never saw, but who sent me gold, with a request that I should pray for him in Jerusalem. Now, O Lord, let blessings come upon him from an unexpected quarter, and let his basket be filled, and his storehouse abound with plenty, and let not the good things of the earth be his only portion, but let him be found among those to whom it shall be said, "Thou hast been faithful over a few things, and I will make thee a ruler over many."

O my Father in heaven! I now ask Thee in the name of Jesus to remember Zion, with all her Stakes and with all her assemblies. She has been grievously afflicted and smitten; she has mourned; she has wept; her enemies have triumphed and have said, "Ah, where is Thy God?" Her Priests and Prophets have groaned in chains and fetters within the gloomy walls of prisons, while many were slain and now sleep in the arms of death. How long, O Lord, shall iniquity triumph, and sin go unpunished?

Do Thou arise in the majesty of Thy strength and make bare Thine arm in behalf of Thy people. Redress their wrongs and turn their sorrow into joy. Pour the spirit of light and knowledge, grace and wisdom, into the hearts of her Prophets, and clothe her priests with salvation. Let light and knowledge march forth through the empire of darkness, and may the honest in heart flow to their standard, and join in the march to go forth to meet the bridegroom.

Let a peculiar blessing rest upon the Presidency of Thy Church, for at them are the arrows of the enemy directed. Be Thou to them a sun and a shield, their strong tower and hiding place; and in the time of distress and danger be Thou near to deliver. Also the quorum of the Twelve, do Thou be pleased to stand by them for Thou knowest the obstacles which they have to encounter, the temptations to which they are exposed, and the privations which they must suffer. Give us [the Twelve] therefore, strength according to our day, and help us to bear a faithful testimony of Jesus and His Gospel, to finish with fidelity and honor the work which Thou hast given us to do, and then give us a place in Thy glorious kingdom. And let this blessing rest upon every faithful officer and member of Thy Church. And all the glory and honor will we ascribe unto God and the lamb forever and ever. Amen.

Appendix 2

A Passage from the Midrash on Psalm Nine

The Midrash is an extensive genre of Jewish literature, dating from the time of the Talmud to the early Middle Ages, that was devoted to interpreting the Bible either to clarify points of Halachah or for homiletic purposes, to illustrate moral, spiritual, and theological points. The rabbinic sages who composed the Midrash utilized some unique methods in interpreting the Bible. This typical selection from the Midrash is included in the appendix for a number of reasons.

1. It illustrates the rabbinic play on words in the Hebrew text. This is found in the first paragraph, where *ha'olam* is read as *ha'olelim*.

2. It illustrates how the rabbis would give a word (*ha'olam*) more than one meaning in their exegetical interpretations.

3. It illustrates how the rabbis could find additional meaning in a word because of how it is spelled.

4. It illustrates that the rabbis had no difficulty in finding numerous interpretations for a single verse, and thus that there was no one absolute interpretation but there

could be both/and interpretations, any of which might be acceptable in a given situation.

5. There is a reference to the inclination to evil, the *yetzer ha'ra*. Since Judaism believes that people are born basically good, there has to be a reason why they sometimes do bad things. The rabbis taught that there is a good and an evil inclination within every human being. However, as they point out in this Midrash, the inclination to evil can be harnessed for good purposes; here it is the sexual urge, which might lead to rape or sodomy, but when used for good leads to marriage and the nurturing of the family. This reflects the Jewish view that one can sanctify life by properly using what might otherwise be evil if improperly used.

6. It refers to the year or day of redemption, one of the rabbinic terms for the messianic era.

7. It illustrates Judaism's use of additional names for God; in this instance, "the Holy One, blessed be He."

8. The rabbis of the Midrash spoke about the rituals of the Temple in Jerusalem (in this passage the sacrifice of the red heifer) as if it were still in existence in their time, though it had been destroyed a number of centuries earlier.

In the translation given below, words quoted from Scripture are printed in italic to facilitate understanding of the midrash. In addition, the Hebrew words are often provided in transliteration in order to illustrate the rabbinic word-plays.

1. *For the leader: 'alemut libban* (Psalm 9:1):[1] The phrase *'alemut libban* is to be understood in the light of the verse *He hath made everything beautiful in its time; He hath set the world (ha'olam)* in their hearts (*belibbam*) (Ecclesiastes 3:11). R. (Rabbi) Berechiah said in the name of R. Jonathan: Do not read *ha'o-lam*, "the world," but *ha'olelim,* "the little children"; the verse means, therefore, that God has set love of little children in their fathers' hearts. For example, there was a king who had two sons, one grown up, and the other a little one. The grown-up one was scrubbed clean, and the little one was covered with dirt, but the king loved the little one more than he loved the grown-up one.

In a different reading of *He hath set ha'olam in their heart,* R. Jonathan said: God has set the fear of the unknown (*ha'olam*) angel of death in their hearts.

Rab, the son of Samuel, said in the name of Samuel: In the verse *And God saw every thing that He made, and behold, it was very good* (Genesis 1:31), the words *very good* refer to the inclination-to-evil in a man's heart. But how can the inclination-to-evil be termed *very good*? Because Scripture teaches that were it not for the inclination-to-evil, a

---

[1]In the King James Version, this phrase is rendered as "To the chief Musician upon Muth-lab-ben." The meaning of the untranslated Hebrew term was and remains uncertain, and this provides the impetus for the midrashic analysis.

man would not take a wife, nor beget children with her, and so the world could not endure.

In another interpretation, the verse is read *He hath caused to be hidden from their hearts.* The word *ha'olam* being written defectively, without the letter *waw* ("caused to be hidden"); that is, the Holy One, blessed be He, hid the day of death and the day of judgment from the hearts of His creatures. Therefore David said: "Because Thou hidest them from me, I shall sing a Psalm, *For the leader; alemut libban* (Ps 9:1), in praise of Thy hiding of the day of death and the day of judgment from the heart."

2. Another comment on *alemut libban* ("concealed from the heart"). The phrase is to be read in the light of the verse *Koheleth sought to understand the ordinances of delight* (Ecclesiastes 12:10). This verse means that Solomon sought to have God explain to him the scriptural ordinances concerning the red heifer whose ashes were used for lustration [purification], especially the ordinance which R. Isaac stated as follows: "All that have the care of the heifer make their garments unclean, but the heifer itself made clean the unclean." Whereupon the Holy One, blessed be He, quoted the conclusion of the verse *That which was written was upright, even ordinances of truth* (ibid.), and said: "For thy benefit, I wrote long ago in the Book of the Upright, as it is said, *Is this not written in the*

Book of the Upright? (Joshua 10:13): Live uprightly. Live simply. Live faithfully. When I have issued a decree, or established an ordinance, it is not to be questioned, as it is said *This is the ordinance of the Torah which the Lord hath commanded* (Numbers 19:2)."

What is meant here by *This? This* is meant to stress the fact that the series of ordinances concerning the red heifer differs from that concerning the sacrificial heifer, which the elders of a city are ordained to take into a rough valley, and there break its neck.

Another comment on *Koheleth sought to understand,* etc. Solomon sought to have God explain to him the regard for study of Torah, of which we are told, *She is more precious than rubies; and all the things thou canst desire are not to be compared to her* (Proverbs 3:15).

The Holy One, blessed be He, quoted Solomon the conclusion of the verse *That which was written was upright, even words of truth* (Ecclesiastes 12:10), and said: *Since the beginning of the world men have not heard . . . neither hath the eye seen, O God, beside Thee, what He hath prepared for him that waiteth for Him* (Isaiah 64:3).

Another comment: Solomon sought to have God explain to him what is the reward of men who fear God and who trust in Him, men to whom Scripture says: *Ye shall be a delightsome land*

(Malachi 3:12). Thereupon the Holy One, blessed be He, quoted Solomon *That which was written,* etc., and said: "Long ago I wrote: *Oh, how abundant is the goodness which Thou hast laid up for them that fear Thee* (Psalms 31:20)."

Another comment: Solomon sought to have God explain to him what is the reward of acts of mercy, of which God says, *I desire mercy and not sacrifice* (Hosea 6:6). Thereupon the Holy One, blessed be He, quoted Solomon *That which was written,* etc., and said, "Long ago I wrote *Know therefore that the Lord thy God, He is God; the faithful God who keepeth covenant and mercy with them that love Him and keep His commandments* (Deuteronomy 7:9)."

Another comment: Solomon sought to have God explain to him when the year of redemption would come, the year of which we read, *I charge you . . . not to stir up, nor awaken love, till He desire* (Song of Songs 3:5). Thereupon the Holy One, blessed be He, quoted *That which was written,* etc., and said: "Long ago I wrote: *The day of vengeance shall be in My heart until My year of redemption will come* (Isaiah 63:4)."

R. Samuel taught in the name of R. Judah: If a man tells you when the day of redemption is coming, do not believe him, for it is written, *the day of vengeance shall be in My heart* (Isaiah 63:4). If the heart does not disclose its secrets to the mouth, how can the mouth disclose anything?

R. Berechiah and R. Simon, in the name of R. Joshua ben Levi, maintained that the Holy One, blessed be He, said to Solomon: "For thy benefit I supplied three clues to the sepulcher of Moses, as it said, *And He buried him in the valley, in the land of Moab, over against Beth-peor* (Deuteronomy 34:6). Yet in spite of all, *No man knoweth of his sepulcher unto this day* (ibid.). Though I provided so many clues in this matter, no man has been able to solve it: how much more unlikely, then, is the discovery of the time of redemption, of which it is said *The words are closed up and sealed till the time of the end* (Daniel 2:9)."

There is a great deal more to this Midrash, but I believe that these passages will give the reader an idea of the nature of the literature: that it is non-systematic and non-definitive, that it quotes freely from various sections of the Bible to illustrate its points, and that it can encompass a both/and outlook in its approach to Jewish thought.

Appendix 3

The Responsa Literature

The responsa literature, a body of questions and answers on Jewish law, constitutes the rabbinic way of addressing halachic issues, many of which have ethical import. The following two selections, quoted from *Contemporary Reform Responsa* by Rabbi Solomon B. Freehof (Cincinnati: Hebrew Union College Press, 1974), will give the reader an idea of the nature of this literature, demonstrating that it is far from absolutist and is willing to encompass more than one view on the question asked.

The selections illustrate the rabbinical approach to ethical questions. While the specific issues treated may not be of burning moment to the Mormon reader, they raise important ethical concerns nonetheless. In each illustration someone asks for guidance in dealing with a serious real-life problem that presents an ethical dilemma, and Rabbi Freehof responds by searching the Jewish legal sources to find insights which cast their light upon the question at hand. The first selection deals with sterilizing the feebleminded, the second, with garnisheeing wages. The brief footnotes identifying the sources cited will give the reader a sense of the ongoing continuity of Jewish ethical discussion over the centuries.

STERILIZING THE FEEBLEMINDED
Question:

A public service organization in a southern state sterilized a feebleminded young girl who was a client of the organization. After the operation was performed, the mother of the girl strongly protested, on the ground that when the authorities suggested to the girl that she be sterilized, she did not understand what was being asked of her. The mother's protest soon became a public agitation. The question is asked: What is the attitude of Jewish law and tradition to this action and to the protest against it? (Asked by R.G., Tallahassee, Florida.)

Answer:

Jewish law is quite definite about the status of the feebleminded (*Shota*) with regard to family relationships. (See the description of the feebleminded in *Hagiga* 3b–4a).[2] It is a definite law that a feebleminded person, like a person who is definitely insane, cannot legally contract marriage (b. *Yebamos* 112b: *Even Hoezer* 44:2).[3] While the specific reason mentioned (in the Talmud) for the inability of the feebleminded to contract legal marriage is based on the

---

[2] *Hagiga* is a tractate of the Talmud.

[3] *Yebamos* is also a talmudic tractate (the small *b.* is an abbreviation for "Babylonian Talmud"). *Even Hoezer* is one of the four divisions of the *Shulchan Aruch*, the standard code of Jewish law, dating from the sixteenth century.

fact that it is dangerous for a normal person to live with such a person, the basic reason must be that the express purpose of marriage is to procreate children. The law is clear that every man is in duty bound by Jewish law to marry and have children (*Even Hoezer* 1:1). While it is true that the great Polish legalist, Isserles,[4] says that nowadays we do not insist that a man should not marry a woman who *cannot* bear children, nevertheless the basic law remains that the purpose of marriage, its mandate, is to "increase and multiply." If, therefore, according to Jewish law a feebleminded person cannot legally contract marriage, it follows logically that they are not meant to have children. Since there may be no marriage for the feebleminded, they may not have children. Of course the law does not deal with or advocate procreation without marriage.

But this fact that the feebleminded may not have children is not necessarily any justification for the social service office to have sterilization performed on a feebleminded person. There is a general Jewish law dealing with sterilization. It is based on Leviticus 22:24, which declares that mutilated animals should not be brought to the altar as sacrifices. Then the verse concludes: "Thou shalt not do so in thy land," upon which the Talmud bases the clear-cut prohibition of any act of sterilization anywhere against animals or humans. So the prohibition is recorded in the law, *Even Hoezer* 4:12, 14. Therefore an observant Jewish

---

[4]Rabbi Moses Isserles (1525–1572) wrote a series of glosses on the *Shulhan Aruch*.

doctor would be prohibited by Jewish law from sterilizing any human being or, for that matter, a Jewish veterinarian would be prohibited from performing a similar operation upon cattle or birds.

While the law seems absolute, there are some mitigations of it. Maimonides (*Issure Biah* 16:2, 6, 9)[5] in discussing the further prohibition that a eunuch, i.e. a sterilized person, may not contract legal marriage, makes this distinction: that if it is because of the patient's sickness that a doctor sterilizes him or her, such a person *may* contract legal marriage. While some disagree with this statement of Maimonides (*Tur, Even Hoezer* 5),[6] he remains a strong authority and most scholars agree with him on this matter. Furthermore, Isserles to 5:14 states that if it is a matter of health, the operation is permitted.

If, therefore, it could be demonstrated that it was for the physical and mental health of this feebleminded girl not to bear children, or not to have the responsibility of raising children, this might be further mitigation of the general prohibition against sterilization.

There is also another possible permissiveness involved. The law against sterilization applies more strictly against males than sterilizing females, because the Biblical command to "increase and multiply" is understood to be directed at men. It is a *man's* obligation to marry. He com-

---

[5]*Issure Biah* is one of the subdivisions of the *Mishneh Torah*, a halachic code compiled by Maimonides in the twelfth century.

[6]The *Tur*, also known as the *Arba'ah Turim*, is a halachic code compiled in the fourteenth century by Rabbi Jacob ben Asher.

mits a sin if he remains a bachelor. A woman commits no sin if she remains a spinster. Therefore the law states (*Even Hoezer* 5:12) that it is prohibited to administer a sterilizing medicine to a man, but a woman may take such a medication (cf. *Chelkas M'chokek* ad loc.).[7] So one authority, Rabad, to *Sifra Emor,* section 5,[8] says that there is no objection to sterilizing a woman medically, but there is objection to sterilizing surgically. Furthermore, Yechiel Epstein, in the *Aruch Ha-Shulchan* to *Even Hoezer* 5 (22),[9] says that the sterilization of women is not forbidden biblically but only as a cautionary measure (i.e. rabbinically) and then he says at the end of section 23, speaking here of both men and women, that if the operation is indispensable for the person's health, it may be done.

One of the legal scholars calls attention to the different forms of the verb "give" in both halves of the law. One may not "give" the medicine to a man, but it does not say "one may not give" the medicine to a woman. It says "a woman may drink the medicine," which means "of her own accord," or "with her consent." In other words, the sterilization would be more defensible in the law if this

---

[7] The *Chelkas M'chokek* is a seventeenth-century commentary on the *Shulhan Aruch* by Rabbi Moses Lima.

[8] Rabad is an acronym for Rabbi Abraham ben David of Posquières (1125–1198). *Sifra* is the Midrash on the Book of Leviticus. In the annual cycle of Torah readings, *Emor* is the designation for Leviticus 21:1–24:23.

[9] The *Aruch ha-Shulhan* is a nineteenth-century commentary on the *Shulhan Aruch.*

feebleminded girl gave her consent, or if she cannot understand what is asked of her, if her parent or guardian gave consent.

To sum up: The law forbidding marriage to the feebleminded implies forbidding them to have children. However, the act of sterilization is forbidden by Jewish law, although the prohibition applies less strictly to women than men. An exception to this prohibition may well be made when health is involved and effective consent is given. If these limitations are observed, it would be safe to say that Jewish legal tradition would not oppose the sterilization of the feebleminded.

GARNISHEEING WAGES
Question:

If the court orders the wages due to an employee to be garnisheed, and the employer is Jewish, has the employer the moral and religious duty to resist the court order, since the Bible prohibits withholding the wages of an employee? (Asked by Rabbi Joshua O. Haberman, Washington, D.C.)

Answer:

The Bible is specific in prohibiting the withholding of wages due to an employee (see Leviticus 19:13 and Deuteronomy 24:16). If, for example, the employee is a day-by-day laborer, he must be paid on the very day that his work is finished. This law is developed in full detail in the Talmud in *Baba Metzia* from 110b to 112b:[10] and

---

[10] *Baba Metzia* is a tractate of the Talmud.

based upon the Talmud, the law is discussed fully by
Maimonides in his *Yad*,[11] in the laws of "hiring" (*S'chiros*),
Chapter 11. Then it is dealt with in the *Tur, Choshen
Mishpot* #339 and the same reference in the *Shulchan
Aruch*.

There are certain circumstances under which even the
strict Jewish law does not deem it a sin to withhold wages.
According to some opinions it is no sin to do so in the
case of agricultural labor (evidently because the farmer
himself gets his money only after the harvest. See the *Tur*).
Also, if the workingman knows beforehand that his
employer has no money except on market-days, then in
that case, the employer is not liable for his delay till the
market-day. Finally, the employer is never liable if the
employee does not demand his wages. This is clearly stated in *Baba Metzia* 12a and in the *Tur* and in the *Shulchan
Aruch* 339:10.

So it may well happen that the employee, whose wages
are garnisheed by the law, may well appreciate the fact that
his employer cannot violate the court order; and knowing
that fact, he does not make the futile gesture of demand-
ing his wages. Thus if he does not demand it (for whatever reason) the employer has committed no sin under
Jewish law if he withholds the wages.

As to the moral principle involved, that may depend
upon what sort of debt it is, for the payment of which the
wages are now being garnisheed. In the Commonwealth

---

[11] *Yad* is another name for the *Mishneh Torah* of Maimonides, cited in
the preceding responsum.

of Pennsylvania, for example, we have no garnisheeing of wages, except for the support of children and a wife (also for income tax). If it is to support children and a wife, how could it be considered unethical for the employer to help in their support in this regard?

There is another ethical consideration involved. The sin denounced in Scripture actually involves two sins: (a) the workman is deprived of what he has justly earned and (b) the employer dishonestly keeps (permanently or for a time) money belonging to the worker. But in the case of the garnisheeing of the wages to pay a debt (to a third party) while it is true that the workman is deprived of his just due, the employer at least does not have the use of the money withheld. It goes to satisfy the debt designated in the writ.

But actually the whole question is theoretical. The garnisheeing of wages comes to the employer as a court order which he cannot fail to obey without legal penalty. The fact that he is compelled to obey the court order has special relevance in Jewish law. In all matters of civil law (such as these) the principle of *Dina D'malchusa Dina* applies, "The law of the land is the law." In such cases it is the duty (the *Jewish* duty) of the employer to obey the law. This principle of *Dina D'malchusa Dina* does not apply in ritual or spiritual matters. A decree to violate Jewish law in such matters should be resisted even to martyrdom. But the decrees of a secular court in *civil* matters are laws which (by Jewish law) we are bound to obey. Therefore the employer has no moral or *religious* right to pay the man his wages.

Used by Permission

Glossary of Words (Jewish Chapters)

1) *Akedah*–Genesis 22, the story of the binding of Isaac

2) *B'rit*–Covenant–also pronounced b'ris, or b'rit- refers usually to the covenant between God and the Jewish people

3) *B.C.E.*–Before the Common Era–since Jews do not accept Jesus, the term B.C. (Before Christ) is not used

4) *C.E.*–Common Era–used instead of A.D., *anno domini*–the Year of our Lord

5) *Challah*–a braided egg bread used to welcome the Sabbath and other special holidays (except Passover)

6) *Gemara*–rabbinic commentary on the *Mishnah* (see below), which together combine to make the *Talmud* (see below also)

7) *Haggadah*–part of the Oral Torah containing sermonic interpretations about the biblical text. It is also the name of the prayerbook used for the Passover Seder

8) *Halachah*–the word used to describe Jewish law - it is best understood as the "way" in which one ought to live and has a far greater scope of meaning than the English word "law"

9) *Havdalah*–the brief ceremony marking the conclusion of the Sabbath on Saturday evening

10) *Kabbalah*–the mystical tradition within Judaism, the best known work of which is the *Zohar*

11) *Kaddish*—a doxology (hymn of praise) found in the worship service, with the one at the conclusion of the worship designated as a mourner's prayer

12) *Kiddush*—the blessing over the wine, recited at many special occasions such as welcoming the Sabbath, at *Havdalah*, as part of the Seder, etc.

13) *Kosher*—ritually fit, usually used with food, but can also apply to a witness in a rabbinic court or to clothing

14) *Midrash*—rabbinic exegesis of the Bible, most often verse by verse on the books of the Bible

15) *Mikveh*—ritual bath used for conversion and ritual purification purposes

16) *Mishnah*—rabbinic commentary on the Bible, primarily of a halachic nature, combined with *Gemara* to make up the *Talmud* (see below)

17) *Mitzvah*—literally a "commandment" but better understood as a religious obligation or responsibility- including worship, charity, being present at happy and sad occasions etc.

18) *Oral Torah*—the rabbinic tradition of biblical interpretation, includes both the *Halachah* and the *Haggadah*

19) *Pentateuch*—the Five Books of Moses, the *Written Torah* (see below)

20) *Pharisees*—the post biblical Jewish group that originally developed the Oral Torah method of interpreting the Bible

21) *Rabbi*—the title of Jewish leaders that came into use after the destruction of the second Temple by the Romans in 70 C.E.

22) *Responsa*–Literature in which a rabbi responds to a halachic question dealing with a specific situation of a novel nature

23) *Shofar*–rams horn used in the Bible and still used on Rosh Hashanah and Yom Kippur

24) *Siddur*–the Jewish prayer book used on week days and the Sabbath

25) *Talmud*–the Mishnah plus the *Gemara* plus additional commentaries, a major source of the Oral Torah

26) *Torah*–the first five books of the Bible but also used as a generic to mean all Jewish learning

27) *Tzedakah*–literally "justice" or "righteousness"–the Hebrew word used to connote "charity"

28) *Written Torah*–first five books of the Bible, and by implication the remainder of the Bible as well

Glossary of Terms (Mormon Chapters)

Aaronic Priesthood:

Also known as, but infrequently called, the Levitical Priesthood. Within the Church of Jesus Christ of Latter-day Saints it is considered to be the lesser priesthood.

Agency:

Sometimes referred to as "free" agency. It is the freedom and ability to choose between good and evil.

Baptism for the dead:

Baptism by proxy performed in Latter-day Saint temples for those who have died.

Bishop:

The leader of a local congregation of Latter-day Saints, known as a ward.

Bishopric:

The bishop and his two counselors

Bishop's storehouse:

A place where foodstuffs and clothing are stored, to be distributed to those in need.

Blessing:

Words of comfort and/or healing, typically given by one holding the higher or Melchizedek Priesthood.

Branch:

The smallest organized unit of the Church. It usually consists of less than 150 active members in areas where there are fewer numbers of Church members. A branch is presided over by a branch president and his two counselors.

Book of Abraham:

One of the Latter-day Saint Scriptures. It makes up a portion of a larger Scripture, the Pearl of Great Price.

Book of Mormon :

The keystone of the Church of Jesus Christ of Latter-day Saints. It is the record of a group of Jews who left Jerusalem ca 600 B.C. and traveled to the American continent.

Book of Moses:
Another part of the Pearl of Great Price.

Brother:
A form of address to a male member of the Church

"Calling":

The term used to indicate the position or responsibility that someone holds in the Church. The person is "called" to that position by inspiration given to one with the authority to make the calling.

Celestial Kingdom:

The highest of the three degrees—or kingdoms—of glory to which one can attain in the afterlife. The goal of all Latter-day Saints.

Chastity–law of:

A commitment made by Latter-day Saints that they shall have no sexual relations with anyone other than with their lawfully wedded husbands or wives.

Council in Heaven:

A council attended by all of the spirit children of God in their pre-mortal state. The purpose was to hear and accept the Father's plan for the creation of the earth and the mortal experience.

Deacon:

One of the offices in the Aaronic priesthood. Usually held by boys 12-14.

Degree of Glory:

Any one of the three post-resurrection kingdoms which an individual may merit in the afterlife. Not to be confused with the post-mortal spirit afterlife which precedes the physical resurrection.

Dispensation of Time:

Also called a gospel dispensation. Latter-day Saints usually refer to the present one as the "dispensation of the fullness of time" preceding the Second Coming of Jesus Christ, the Messiah.

Doctrine and Covenants (D. & C.):

One of the four Latter-day Saint Standard Works. The others are the Bible, the Book of Mormon, and the Pearl of Great Price. The D. & C. is a compilation of the canonized revelations given to Joseph Smith and his successors in the presidency of the Church.

Elder:

Elder is the proper title given to all holders of the Melchizedek Priesthood. It is also a specific office within that priesthood. All general authorities of the Church, as well as all of those men serving full time missions for the Church are addressed as "Elder."

Elias:

A title for one who is a forerunner or preparer, as in John the Baptist as a forerunner for Jesus the Messiah. Also a man called Elias who appeared, with others, to Joseph Smith and Oliver Cowdery in a vision in the Kirtland, Ohio temple on April 3, 1836.

Endowment:

One of the ceremonies performed in Latter-day Saint temples.

Eternal Life:

Literally "God's life." It is the kind of life the Eternal Father in Heaven leads. Not to be confused with immortality.

Exaltation:

A term sometimes used to refer to salvation in the Celestial Kingdom, or Eternal Life.

Family Home Evening:

A family gathering usually held on Monday evenings. The purpose may be spiritual, recreational, or both.

Fast offering:

Monies offered to the bishop of the ward for the purpose of aid to those in need. Typically it represents the money which would otherwise be spent for two meals each month, but if circumstances permit it may be much more generous.

Fast and Testimony Sunday:

The first Sunday of each month. Typically this is the day that Latter-day Saints fast for two meals. During the fast members bear their testimonies to each other during the Sacrament meeting.

First Presidency:

The President of the Church of Jesus Christ of Latter-day Saints and his two counselors.

Foreordination:

To be ordained to fulfill an earthly mission in the pre-mortal spirit world, e.g. to be a prophet (Jer.1:5)

General Authority:

A man called to serve full time to administer the affairs of the Church.

Godhead:

God the Father, God the Son, and God the Holy Ghost. Each is a distinct and separate personage.

Gospel:

Literally "God story" or "good news." The gospel of Jesus Christ is the plan of eternal salvation.

Henotheism:

The belief in or worship of only one God, while not denying the existence of others.

High Council:

In each stake of the Church a *high council* composed of twelve high priests is organized to serve as a judicial and administrative body.

High priest:

An office within the Melchizedek Priesthood. The President of the Church of Jesus Christ of Latter-day Saints is the Presiding High Priest of the Church.

Home teacher:

One who is called to visit a family or single member at least monthly. Ideally, a spiritual lesson is taught during the visit.

House of Israel:

All of the descendants of Jacob's twelve sons. Latter-day Saints consider that they are part of that heritage either literally or by adoption.

Immortality:

A free gift given to all men and women through the death and resurrection of Jesus Christ. All will be resurrected and live forever. Not to be confused with Eternal Life.

Joseph Smith:

The young prophet called by God in 1820.

Joseph Smith Translation (JST)

The prophet Joseph Smith's inspired translation of portions of the Bible.

Lamanites:

The less righteous people of the Book of Mormon

"Living Soul":

When the pre-mortal spirit personality is joined to the mortal body a "living soul" results.

Lucifer/Satan:

A powerful spirit son of God who rebelled against Him and was cast out of heaven, together with those who followed him.

Melchizedek Priesthood:

The higher priesthood, as opposed to the lesser, or Aaronic Priesthood.

Messiah:

The Annointed One—Jesus Christ

Moroni:

A resurrected being who lived on the American continent ca 400 AD. He buried and later delivered to Joseph Smith the gold plates upon which the Book of Mormon was written.

Nephites:

The more righteous people of the Book of Mormon

Paradise:

That portion of the post-mortal spirit world to which the righteous are assigned prior to their resurrection.

Patriarch:

Two high priests are generally called from within each stake of the Church to be *stake patriarchs.* They are chosen and ordained to the position for life. Their special assignment is to give partriachal blessings to members of the Church. Not to be confused with the biblical patriarchs.

Pearl of Great Price:

One of the four standard works, or Scriptures, of the Church.

Pre-existence:

The pre-mortal spirit world where all spirit children of God lived before coming to earth and receiving mortal bodies.

Plan of Salvation:

The plan accepted by the spirit children of God in the pre-mortal Council in Heaven. Otherwise known as the Gospel of Jesus Christ, it provides a means by which all spirit children may return after their mortal lives to dwell with God.

Priesthood:

Priesthood is the power and authority delegated to men to act for God on the earth. It may also refer to the men of the Church in general.

Priest:

One of the offices of the Aaronic Priesthood. Usually held by young men 16 and over or by adult converts to the Church prior to their receiving the Melchizedek Priesthood.

Quorum of the Twelve:

The Quorum of the Twelve Apostles. The senior member of the Quorum by length of service is the president of the Quorum of the Twelve and normally becomes the next president and prophet of the Church upon the death of the current president.

Reformed Egyptian:

The language in which the Book of Mormon was written. Assumed to be a shorthand for Hebrew.

Relief Society:

The women's organization in the Church.

Revelation:

The making known of divine truth to man by communication from the heavens..

Sacrament:

During Sunday Sacrament meeting Latter-day Saints partake of bread and water. By partaking of the sacrament they renew the covenant previously made by them in the waters of baptism.

Sealings, sealer:

As part of the temple ordinances, Latter-day Saints are "sealed" to their spouses, parents and children as part of an eternal continuum in the afterlife. This is done both for the living and for the dead.. The ordinance is performed by a one having the authority to do so and who is called a "sealer." The sealing ordinances are considered to be the crowning ordinances of the gospel.

Seventy:
This term implies a special call to preach the gospel. Most general authorities of the Church are members of one of the Quorums of Seventies.

Sister:
A form of address to female members of the Church. Also the title of full-time female missionaries.

Spirit Prison:
That portion of the post-mortal spirit world to which the wicked are consigned prior to being resurrected.

Stake:
Referred to as a "stake of Zion." An organizational unit consisting of a number of individual congregations or wards. Presided over by a stake president and two counselors known as the "stake presidency."

Teacher:
An office in the Aaronic Priesthood. Typically held by boys age 14-16.

Telestial kingdom:
The lowest of the three degrees of glory in the afterlife.

Temple:

A building where sacred ordinances are performed both for the living and the dead.

Terrestrial kingdom:

The intermediate of the three degrees of glory in the afterlife.

Temple marriage:

A sealing ordinance whereby couples are joined to each other for both time and eternity.

Visiting Teacher:

A sister called by the Relief Society to visit the home of another sister.

Ward:

The name of the local congregation—usually consisting of at least 150-200 members.

Word of Wisdom:

A law of health given by revelation. It proscribes the use of alcohol, tobacco, tea, and coffee.